OUR GUILTY SILENCE

D0913267

The Reverend John R. W. Stott, M.A., Q.H.C., Rector of All Souls Church, Langham Place, London, has also written:

MEN WITH A MESSAGE
BASIC CHRISTIANITY
YOUR CONFIRMATION
WHAT CHRIST THINKS OF THE CHURCH
THE PREACHER'S PORTRAIT
CONFESS YOUR SINS
THE EPISTLES OF JOHN
THE CANTICLES AND SELECTED PSALMS
MEN MADE NEW

OUR GUILTY SILENCE

JOHN R. W. STOTT

WILLIAM B. EERDMANS PUBLISHING COMPANY
Grand Rapids, Michigan

Copyright © 1967 by the Evangelical Fellowship in the
Anglican Communion

Fourth printing, July 1974

ISBN 0-8028-1287-2

INTRODUCTION

IN a day when the Church's evangelistic mission was never more urgent it would seem that the Church's evangelistic enterprise was never more lacking or ineffective. One might almost say that the contemporary Church is better equipped for every other task than for its primary responsibility of making known the gospel of Christ and winning others to Him. It is certainly true that the Church as a whole displays more enterprise in other fields (for example, in theological debate, liturgical reform and social service) than in the realm of evangelism. Indeed the very word evangelism has almost dropped out of currency, except in a debased form. In certain quarters the whole thing is looked upon with ill-disguised scepticism and suspicion. Some openly admit—if not actually boast—that they do not know what the evangel is. Others question the necessity of conversion, or deny that it is the Church's job to convert anyone. Yet others feebly substitute some form of humanitarianism for positive and aggressive Christian witness.

In face of so much confusion, hesitation and weakness the present book offers a vigorous challenge to the Church to recover its evangelistic vision and embark afresh on its evangelistic mission. And this of necessity must involve proclamation, testimony, sharing the good news. The author is convinced that the Church when it is true to its calling cannot be a silent Church. As he says, 'If the gospel is the good news it claims to be, and if it has been entrusted to us, we incur guilt if we do not pass it on.' Hence the title of the work.

One of the values of the book is that it comes from the

pen of one who has consistently put evangelism in the forefront of his work throughout his ordained ministry. He has also had an exceptionally wide experience in this field, both in parochial evangelism within the sphere of his own congregation at All Souls, Langham Place, London, and in student evangelism through university missions in various parts of the world. Out of his own ministry and experience he speaks in urgent tones to the Church of today and seeks to recall it to what is at once the most difficult, the most important, and the most glorious of all enterprises.

PHILIP E. HUGHES
FRANK COLQUHOUN

CONTENTS

AUTHOR'S PREFACE

In June 1945 a famous report was published in Britain. It was the work of a special Commission on Evangelism appointed by the Archbishops of Canterbury and York, and was entitled *Towards the Conversion of England*.

In describing the part of the laity in evangelism, the report mentions reticence as one of the hindrances, 'shyness in speaking about the things of God'. 'We cannot exaggerate the importance of breaking down this traditional English reserve which produces a Church of "silent saints". As Prebendary Wilson Carlile (who coined this phrase) declared: "I have got the biggest job I have ever tackled in my life. I am trying to open the mouths of the people in the pews".'[1]

It is the theme of this little book that such silence is *guilty silence*. Of course, 'there is a time to be silent', but there is also 'a time to speak'.[2] If the gospel is the 'good news' it claims to be, and if it has been entrusted to us, we incur guilt if we do not pass it on. Like those Samaritan lepers who found the Syrian army camp was abandoned, we need to acknowledge our guilt and say: 'We are doing wrong. This is a day of good news, yet we are holding our tongues!'[3]

Not that this guilt is by any means confined to the laity. Many of us clergy are tongue-tied too. Let me give you an up-to-date personal example. In order to write these

1 pp. 51-53.
2 Eccles. 3:7.

9

pages I have come away to a remote corner of Pembroke-shire in South Wales. I travelled by sleeper and found I was sharing the two-berth cabin with a young land agent. He was occupying the top bunk. In the morning, while preparing to wash, he accidentally dropped the contents of his sponge bag on to the floor and vented his annoyance by taking the name of Christ in vain. I said nothing. Indeed, I was sorely tempted to remain silent. The usual plausible excuses came crowding into my head—'it's none of your business', 'you've no responsibility for him', 'he'll only laugh at you'. But the previous evening I had preached in church from Ephesians 4:26, 27: 'Be angry but do not sin'. I had spoken about righteous indignation and the façade of sweet reasonableness which often conceals our moral cowardice and compromise. An inner struggle followed, as I argued with myself and prayed, and not until ten or fifteen minutes later did I find the courage to speak. Although his immediate reaction was unfavourable, I was soon able to witness to the Christ he had blasphemed and to give him an evangelistic booklet.

I suppose this simple anecdote could be paralleled a thousand times. Again and again an opportunity presents itself to speak for our Lord Jesus Christ, but we hold our peace. And what is true of us as individual believers seems to characterize and paralyse the whole Church.

What are the causes of our guilty silence?

No doubt any answer to this question would tend to be an over-simplification, because the reasons are legion. But I believe there are four major causes. Either we have no compelling incentive even to try to speak, or we do not know what to say, or we are not convinced that it is our job, or we do not believe we shall do any good, because

³II Ki. 7:9 (Jerusalem Bible).

we have forgotten the source of power.

These four uncertainties and their remedies form the substance of this book. First, we shall consider the greatest evangelistic incentive, which is concern for *the glory of God*. Next, we shall seek to summarize the evangelistic message or *the gospel of God*. Thirdly, we shall examine the evangelistic agency, which is *the Church of God;* and finally we shall remind ourselves of the only true evangelistic dynamic, namely *the Spirit of God*.

Here and there, as I write, I shall be referring to my own experience of evangelism. This has been largely limited to two kinds—parochial evangelism in the regular work of a local church (All Souls, Langham Place, in London's West End), which it has been my privilege to serve for the twenty-one years since I was ordained, and student evangelism in university missions in various parts of the world. I realize that both types of evangelism are to some extent atypical; yet I believe that the principles which I shall try to illustrate are universally applicable.

It is always hazardous to write from a personal point of view. I shall seek to be honest, before God, and certainly I have no success story to tell. But I write from deepening conviction born of two parents—Scripture and ministry—a careful study of the one and a growing experience of the other.

In the course of preparing the manuscript I have also sought the help of the members of my own congregation by issuing a questionnaire to 'commissioned workers' and 'fellowship groups'. This enquired into the details of their conversion to Christ. A hundred and five people of varied ages and backgrounds completed it, and I am grateful to them for their co-operation. Some of the information gleaned from the enquiry appears on later pages.

CHAPTER ONE

THE GLORY OF GOD

THE EVANGELISTIC INCENTIVE

Most people are talkative. Some seldom stop talking! Why is it then that our flow of speech so quickly dries up when the conversation drifts to religion? Sometimes our silence betrays our lack of Christian conviction and experience. But even when we are sure of the gospel and have known its power in our own lives, we are still inhibited by natural diffidence, by conventional taboos, and by the fear of ridicule or of a rebuff. Only strong, positive incentives will enable us to overcome these resistances.

Politicians, economists and employers, concerned to increase production, pay careful attention to the question of incentives. Some good biblical theology lies behind their study. They seem to recognize that because man is fallen he has a tendency to sloth, and that because he is a rational being he needs to be told not only what to do, but why he should do it. In industry, commerce and the public services a further concession to the Christian doctrine of man is tacitly made, in that the incentives chosen usually take the form of an appeal to self-interest. Attractive rewards are offered—better conditions, higher pay, bigger bonuses, fatter pensions, longer holidays.

In evangelism too we need incentives, for evangelism is difficult and dangerous work. It brings us face to face with

13

the enemy in hand-to-hand combat. It takes us to the frontier with the world, and exposes us to the peril of counter-attack. Some never begin to evangelize for want of adequate incentives. Others begin, but grow discouraged and give up; they need fresh incentives. Others find their evangelism vitiated from the start because they are impelled by false motives. There is a great need for the Church to be purged of wrong motives and fired by right ones.

OBEDIENCE AND LOVE

What impels the Christian to be active in witness? The basic motive is plain obedience. Every Christian is a servant of Christ. He has been 'bought with a price'[1] and is now attached to his master by the bonds of a grateful obedience. 'The love of Christ controls us.' It has us in its grip. Indeed, since our new life is due entirely to Christ's death, His love hems us in and 'leaves us no choice' but to live for Him.[2] In seeking to live for Christ we are concerned to do His will and keep His commandments, all of them. We are not at liberty to pick and choose. Nor do we wish to. So we do not overlook His last commandment, to 'go . . . and make disciples.'[3]

Such an emphasis on obedience may seem to imply a spirit of reluctance on our part. This is not so. Not only is obedience the fruit and proof of love, but also—and especially in the command to evangelize—it brings an honourable privilege, since the call of God is to share in His own mission in the world. First, He sent His Son. Then He sent His Spirit. Now He sends His Church, that

[1] I Cor. 6:20; 7:23.
[2] II Cor. 5:14, 15 (RSV and NEB).
[3] Matt. 28:19.

is, us. He sends us out by His Spirit into His world to announce His Son's salvation. He worked through His Son to achieve it; He works through us to make it known.[4]

If loving obedience to God and His Christ is the first evangelistic incentive, loving concern for men is the second. To love my neighbour is to seek and to serve his highest good. Precisely what this is we shall attempt to elucidate in the next chapter. For the moment it is sufficient to say that man's highest good is more than the basic necessities of food, clothing and shelter. It is not even health of body and mind or harmonious integration into society. It concerns his relationship with God, in whose image and likeness he has been made.

It is because man is fundamentally a spiritual being that he cannot live by bread alone. He has a deeper hunger than baker's bread can satisfy. If we know this, and if we also know the gospel which can introduce him to 'the true bread from heaven',[5] we cannot claim to love him if we leave him alone to starve. 'If a brother or sister is ill-clad and in lack of daily food, and one of you says to them, "Go in peace, be warmed and filled", without giving them the things needed for the body, what does it profit?'[6] This question is even more searching when 'the things needed' are not for the body but for the soul. To say this is not to forget that man is one person, a body-soul, or to imply that his physical needs may be ignored. It is rather an assertion that the neglect of my neighbour's spiritual needs, on whatever pretext, is incompatible with the claim to love him. Such neglect is criminal irresponsibility. To suppress the good news in silence is to incur guilt.

[4] See II Cor. 5:18 ('through Christ') and v. 20 ('through us').
[5] Jn. 6:32.
[6] Jas. 2:15, 16.

Compelling as the motives of obedience and compassion are, neither is in fact the strongest evangelistic incentive. What this is we may learn from the apostles Paul and John. At the beginning of his letter to the Romans, describing various aspects of the apostleship he has received from Jesus Christ, Paul writes that his mission to all the nations is 'for the sake of his name'.[7] And John refers to certain missionaries who have set out (literally) 'for the sake of the name'.[8] No possessive adjective tells us for whose name they were so concerned. But we have no difficulty in guessing. It was the pre-eminent name of Jesus. The early Christians, who were proud 'to suffer indignity for the sake of the Name',[9] were eager to evangelize in the same cause. Even love for the commands of Christ and love for the lost sheep of Christ are subordinate to and dependent on this love for the name of Christ.

Love for His name is not a sentimental attachment either to His personal name 'Jesus' or to His official title 'Christ' or to any of His designations in Scripture. Instead, it is a concern for His honour in the world, an ardent desire for the fulfilment of our prayer: 'Not to us, O LORD, not to us, but to thy name give glory'.[10] It is a recognition that God the Father has exalted Him 'far above . . . every name that is named'[11] and indeed 'bestowed on him the name which is above every name', with a view to securing 'that at the name of Jesus', before His supreme rank and dignity, 'every knee should bow . . . and every tongue confess that Jesus Christ is Lord . . .'[12]

[7] Rom. 1:5.
[8] III John 7.
[9] Acts 5:41 (NEB). The expression is the same: *huper tou onomatos*.
[10] Ps. 115:1.
[11] Eph. 1:21.
[12] Phil. 2:9-11.

It comes as a surprise to many people, even as a shock, that this love for the name of God and of Christ is regularly expressed in Scripture in terms of 'jealousy'. Some churchmen are embarrassed during the recitation of the ten commandments at holy communion to hear it said in the second that 'I the Lord thy God am a jealous God.' It seems to them almost intolerable that in the same biblical passage He should be described first as 'a God merciful and gracious' and then as 'a jealous God, whose name is Jealous'.[13] Jealousy is condemned in the Bible as a horrible sin. We know from literature and from experience how it warps human personality and disrupts communities. The apostle Paul specifies it as one of 'the works of the flesh', a product of our fallen nature.[14] How then can it possibly be attributed to the holy God? How can His name be both 'holy' and 'jealous'?[15] Must we write this off as a biblical discrepancy, or is there an alternative explanation?

It is certainly strange that the same word 'jealousy' can denote an attribute of God and a sin of man. But this is because in itself jealousy is neutral. Whether it is good or evil is determined by the situation which arouses it. In essence jealousy is an intolerance of rivals; it is a virtue or a sin according to whether the rival's presence is legitimate or not. Thus, competition in business or in sport is perfectly legitimate. A shop-keeper has no right to resent the success of another retailer who threatens his business, because he cannot claim a monopoly of the local trade. Again, an athlete should not become bitter or jealous when

[13] Exod. 34:6, 14.
[14] Gal. 5:19, 20.
[15] Isa. 57:15; Exod. 34:14.

he is beaten at his own game, because he has no personal right to an undisputed victory. His professional jealousy is but wounded vanity.

Jealousy in marriage, however, is a very different matter, because marriage is a permanently exclusive relationship. Both husband and wife have solemnly vowed that, 'forsaking all other', they will keep only unto their partner, so long as they both shall live. In their married life therefore each will (or should) brook no rival. If a third party intrudes into the marriage, the offended person, whether husband or wife, is right to be jealous. In such a case it is tolerance of the rival, not intolerance, which is sin.

The jealousy of God is usually mentioned in Scripture in the context of His choice of Israel as His bride. His covenant with Israel was a marriage covenant, and in accepting the divine proposal Israel committed herself to entire loyalty and obedience. Her flirtations with the Canaanite Baals, leading to acts of spiritual adultery and even of promiscuous harlotry, were therefore breaches of the covenant. It is these things which are said to have provoked Israel's God to anger and to jealousy.[16]

Yet the ground of the jealousy of God is broader than His covenant relationship with Israel. If it were only this, it would not include the rest of mankind. But God's jealousy is aroused by all forms of idolatry, whoever the idolater may be. Its basis is the creation, not just the covenant. If His very name is 'Jealous', it is not because He is Israel's God, but because He is God, the only living and true God. If He is God and He alone, the sole Creator and Lord of men, He has a right to our exclusive worship

---

[16] Cf. Paul's use of the marriage metaphor and his sense of jealousy in II Cor. 11:1-4.

and is 'jealous' when we misdirect it to idols which are no-gods. 'I am the LORD, and there is no other, besides me there is no God'. 'There is no other god besides me, a righteous God and a Saviour; there is none besides me. Turn to me and be saved, all the ends of the earth! For I am God, and there is no other. By myself I have sworn, from my mouth has gone forth in righteousness a word that shall not return: "To me every knee shall bow, every tongue shall swear".'[17] It is this fact of God as the one and only God which justifies both His demand for the homage of every knee and tongue and His jealousy when it is withheld: 'I am the LORD, that is my name; my glory I give to no other, nor my praise to graven images'.[18]

Monotheism remains the essential basis for mission. The supreme reason why God 'desires *all men* to be saved and come to the knowledge of the (same) truth' is that 'there is *one God*, and there is one mediator between God and men, the man Christ Jesus, who gave himself as a ransom for all . . .'[19] The logic of this passage rests on the relation between 'all men' and 'one God'. Our warrant for seeking the allegiance of 'all men' is that there is only 'one God', and only 'one mediator' between Him and them. Without the unity of God and the uniqueness of Christ there could be no Christian mission.

What the Bible goes on to say is this. If God is right to be 'jealous', to oppose and resist the wickedness of men who do not give to Him the glory due to His name, but turn aside to idols, then His own people should share His jealousy. Indeed, there are examples of this in both the Old and the New Testament. Elijah was wrong in sup-

[17] Isa. 45:5, 21-23.
[18] Isa. 42:8.
[19] I Tim. 2:4-6.

posing that he alone of all his compatriots had not bowed the knee to Baal. But he was right in saying: 'I have been very jealous for the LORD, the God of hosts; for the people of Israel have forsaken thy covenant'.[20] Through the evil influence of Queen Jezebel, who had imported into Israel her father's Phoenician cult, large numbers of the people had become unfaithful to Jehovah. If He was provoked to jealousy by their apostasy, His prophet Elijah was made jealous also.

Perhaps the closest New Testament parallel is to be found in Paul's first visit to Athens. There is something very moving about the great Christian apostle alone amid the glories of ancient Greece. We can picture him wandering through the city, gazing at its famous buildings. Yet what struck him was not the beauty, but the idolatry: 'his spirit was provoked within him as he saw that the city was full of idols'.[21] The provocation he felt was a 'paroxysm' of spirit, a deeply-felt emotion. Luke uses the verb which in the Septuagint frequently describes how God was 'provoked' to anger or jealousy. And what provoked God in Israel is exactly what provoked Paul in Athens— idolatry. Divine jealousy stirred within him as he saw the city's idolatrous worship. 'So he argued . . .'[22] In the synagogue with the religious, in the market-place with casual passers-by, and on the Areopagus with the philosophers the apostle preached the gospel persuasively and indefatigably. It was jealousy for the name of God and of Christ, profaned by heathen idolatry, which gave him his zeal for evangelism. Indeed, 'jealousy' and 'zeal' are the

[20] I Ki. 19:9-18.
[21] Acts 17:16.
[22] Acts 17:17.

same word.[23] He burned with longing that the Athenians should know and honour the God they either ignorantly worshipped or actually by their idolatry denied.

Turning from Scripture to the history of the Christian missionary enterprise, we find the same dominant incentive in the greatest of Christ's ambassadors. It was not only a humble and grateful obedience to Christ's commission which fired them, nor even a vision of the perishing multitudes, but a passionate love for the name of Christ.

The best example I know comes from the biography of Henry Martyn. Although a Senior Wrangler of Cambridge University, and then a Fellow of St. John's College, he turned his back on an academic career and entered the ministry. Two years later, on July 16th, 1805, he sailed for India. 'Let me burn out for God,' he cried in Calcutta, as he lived in an abandoned Hindu temple.[24] And as he watched the people prostrating themselves before their images, he wrote: 'this excited more horror in me than I can well express.'[25]

Later he moved to Shiraz, and busied himself with the translation of the New Testament into Persian. Many Muslim visitors came to see him and to engage him in religious conversation. His customary serenity was only disturbed when anybody insulted his Lord. On one occasion the sentiment was expressed that 'Prince Abbas Mirza had killed so many Christians that Christ from the fourth heaven took hold of Mahomet's skirt to entreat him to desist.' It was a dramatic fantasy. Here was Christ

[23] *Zēlos*. See John 2:17, where Jesus' 'zeal' for God's house was basically a 'jealousy' for His honour and glory.
[24] Constance E. Padwick: *Henry Martyn, Confessor of the Faith* (I.V.F., 1953), p. 87.
[25] *Op cit.*, p. 89.

kneeling before Mahommed. How would Martyn react?
'I was cut to the soul at this blasphemy.' Seeing his discomfiture, his visitor asked what it was that was so offensive. Martyn replied: 'I could not endure existence if Jesus was not glorified; it would be hell to me, if He were to be always thus dishonoured.' His Muslim visitor was astonished and again asked why. 'If anyone pluck out your eyes,' he answered, 'there is no saying *why* you feel pain;—it is feeling. It is because I am one with Christ that I am thus dreadfully wounded.'[26]

I never read these words of Martyn's without being rebuked, for I do not have this passionate love for Christ's honour or feel this acute pain. Nor do I see it much (if at all) in the contemporary Church. But is not this the cause of our guilty silence? We do not speak for Christ because we do not so love His name that we cannot bear to see Him unacknowledged and unadored. If only our eyes were opened to see His glory, and if only we felt wounded by the shame of His public humiliation among men, we should not be able to remain silent. Rather would we echo the apostles' words: 'we cannot but speak of what we have seen and heard.'[27]

WORSHIP AND WITNESS

This incentive of the glory of God is the link between our worship and our witness. It is misleading to divorce them as if they were two quite separate functions of the Church. Rightly understood, they belong together. Professor Douglas Webster has written that 'the two superlative interests of the early Church' were, and indeed the 'two preoccupations' of today's Church should be, 'God and

[26] *Op. cit.*, p. 146.
[27] Acts 4:20.

the outsider' or 'worship and mission'.[28] Our task now is to see how each, if it is true to itself, inevitably involves the other.

First, *worship involves witness*. The factor which unites them is the name of God. For what is worship but to 'glory in His holy name', to 'praise', 'bless' or 'stand in awe of' it?[29] And what is witness but to 'proclaim the name of the Lord' to others?[30] These expressions are found in the Psalter, and it is in the Psalms that the proper combination of worship and witness is most clearly and commonly found.

God had revealed to Israel His name, that is to say, His nature and will.[31] Revelation is essentially a disclosure of the divine name. It was begun through Moses and the prophets, and completed by Jesus Christ who said: 'I have manifested thy name to the men whom thou gavest me out of the world.'[32] Now God's name is frequently called 'holy', meaning that it is 'apart', separate from and supreme over all other names. Indeed, it is the holiness or uniqueness of His name which makes it the only proper object of man's worship. And the more men come to recognize the holiness of God's name, the more they desire God so to 'vindicate' it[33] that everybody else will come to worship Him too: 'let them praise the name of the LORD, for his name alone is exalted; his glory is above heaven and earth.'[34] Worship is 'worth-ship', an acknowledgment of the worth of Almighty God. And God's worth is

[28] *What is Evangelism?* p. 43, and *Local Church and World Mission*, p. 73.
[29] Ps. 105:3. Cf. Pss. 113:1-4; 145:1, 2; Mal. 2:5.
[30] Deut. 32:3. Cf. Ps. 22:22; 45:17; 96:2, 3.
[31] For example, Exod. 33:19; 34:5-8.
[32] John 17:6.
[33] Ezek. 36:22, 23.
[34] Ps. 148:13. Cf. 113:3.

absolute. It is the same for every other man as it is for me, and for me as it is for every other man. It is therefore impossible for me to worship God truly and yet not care two cents whether anybody else worships Him too. Sincerely to pray 'Hallowed be Thy name' is bound to make us witnesses, 'for the sake of the Name', the very name whose hallowing we say we desire.

It is not surprising therefore that it was during a time of worship that the first missionary journey was conceived: 'While they were worshipping the Lord and fasting, the Holy Spirit said, "Set apart for me Barnabas and Saul for the work to which I have called them".'[35] Worship which does not beget mission is hypocrisy. We cannot acclaim the worth of God if we have no desire to proclaim it.

One can sympathize with young Hudson Taylor in Brighton in June 1865, so burdened for China that he found the self-satisfied, hymn-singing congregation intolerable. He looked round him. 'Pew upon pew of prosperous bearded merchants, shopkeepers, visitors; demure wives in bonnets and crinolines, scrubbed children trained to hide their impatience; the atmosphere of smug piety sickened him. He seized his hat and left. "Unable to bear the sight of a congregation of a thousand or more Christian people rejoicing in their own security, while millions were perishing for lack of knowledge, I wandered out on the sands alone, in great spiritual agony".' And there on the beach he prayed for 'twenty-four willing skilful labourers'.[36]

One can even sympathize with this aspect of the so-

[35] Acts 13:1-3.
[36] John C. Pollock: *Hudson Taylor and Maria* (Hodder and Stoughton, 1962), p. 132 f.

called 'religionless Christianity'. Where religion is without mission, we should prefer mission without religion. But fortunately we are not left with this choice. Worship that is pleasing to God will inevitably send us out to bear witness of the Name we have sought to honour. Indeed, 'worship can henceforth only be authentic if it embraces both the vertical and the horizontal.'[37] We ought perhaps to end our services more often with the form of blessing which begins: 'Go forth into the world . . .' Bolder still are the words which conclude the Roman Mass: *Ite missa est*. They are rendered by some writers as the peremptory command, 'Get out!'[38]

If worship involves witness, it is important also to assert the corollary that *witness involves worship* too. This can best be understood by considering the remarkable sacrificial language which Paul twice uses in relation to evangelism. In the epistle to the Philippians he writes of his longing that his readers will both 'shine as lights in the world' and 'hold forth the word of life'. Only then will he be able to rejoice in the day of Christ that his labours have not been in vain. He goes on to speak of their faith in God as a 'sacrificial offering' to Him. So ardently does he want this their oblation to be acceptable to God, that he says he would even be glad to give his life for them, to be (as it were)'poured as a libation upon' their sacrifice.[39] Although the pictorial background is strange and unfamiliar to us, the general sense is clear. Paul gives to his evangelism a Godward significance. He thinks of his converts' faith and

[37]*Planning for Mission,* p. 186. See the whole section entitled 'Worship and Mission' (pp. 185-192) and the book with this title by J. G. Davies (S.C.M. 1966).
[38]For example, *Local Church and World Mission,* p. 91.
[39]Phil. 2:15-18.

his own labours for them as mingling together in a single sacrifice, an offering of worship to God which is pleasing in His sight.

The apostle employs a similar metaphor in Romans 15:16 in describing his ministry to the nations. He calls himself 'a minister of Christ Jesus to the Gentiles in the priestly service of the gospel of God, so that the offering of the Gentiles may be acceptable, sanctified by the Holy Spirit'. The whole sentence is crammed with sacrificial language and ideas. He thinks of the evangelist as a priest, and of evangelism as 'priestly service'. Now the great function of the Old Testament priesthood was the offering of sacrifices;[40] what sacrifice has the evangelist to offer? Answer: his converts! '. . . that the offering of the Gentiles may be acceptable, sanctified by the Holy Spirit'.

This implies that neither evangelism (the preaching of the gospel) nor its immediate result (the winning of converts) is to be understood as an end in itself. Why do we want to win converts? What do we intend to do with them when they are won? Biblical evangelism never puts a full stop after conversion but regards conversion as the prelude to worship. The evangelist should look beyond the benefit which comes to the convert who is saved to the glory which comes to the God who saves him. Our ultimate aim is to 'offer' converts to God, in the sense that after conversion they offer themselves to Him as worshippers in word and deed. And once the convert becomes a true worshipper, he will find himself driven out again into the world as a witness.

It is in this way that worship and witness involve each other. Each is maimed without the other. Each, if true to

[40] Cf. Heb. 8:3.

itself, leads to the other, thus producing an unending cycle. Worship expresses itself in witness; witness fulfils itself in worship. The unifying theme is the glory of God and of His Christ, and there is a great need for this to be the supreme incentive of our modern evangelism.

> *Let every kindred, every tribe,*
>   *On this terrestrial ball,*
> *To Him all majesty ascribe,*
>   *And crown Him Lord of all.*

CHAPTER TWO

THE GOSPEL OF GOD

THE EVANGELISTIC MESSAGE

The second reason for our guilty silence is that we are neither clear nor sure what we ought to speak. We say nothing because we have nothing to say. Our tongue is tied and our lips are sealed because we lack either a thorough knowledge of the gospel or a conviction about its truth or both. There can be no evangelism without an evangel, no mission without a message.

This has never been more apparent than it is today. Theological indecision is an obvious feature of contemporary Christendom. 'The Church has become confused and uncertain in the proclamation of its message'; 'if the Church would speak with conviction and authority, the nation would gladly hearken'.[1] Moreover, this situation does not escape the notice of onlookers. Professor Douglas Webster quotes a Buddhist monk who said: 'To the eastern religious it looks as if Christianity has reached the stage in adolescence when the child is slightly ashamed of his father and embarrassed when talking about him.'[2]

The chief cause of this dilemma is the rapidity with which modern life is changing. Everything and everybody are on the move; it seems impossible to stand still. The

---

[1] *Towards the Conversion of England*, pp. 16, 15.
[2] *Yes to Mission*, p. 9.

whole world is engulfed in a gigantic revolution, political, economic, social, intellectual. The end of imperialism and the rise of communism, the advances of science and technology, the population explosion, the threat of atomic destruction, the widespread adoption of the concept of social welfare, the renascence of ancient eastern faiths, and the spread of secularist humanism in the west—all these phenomena affect the man in the street and contribute to his sense of uneasy confusion.

Some modern theologians argue that we must have a new gospel for this new world. The old-fashioned gospel will no longer do. It is out of date, irrelevant. It must be discarded and replaced. In contrast to this, it is refreshing to read the view expressed in *Towards the Conversion of England*. At the head of chapter II is William Temple's statement: 'The Gospel is true always and everywhere, or it is not a Gospel at all, or true at all.' A little later the Commission writes: 'It is the *presentation* of the Gospel, not its *content*, that changes with succeeding generations and their varying conditions.'[3]

Others are actually equating evangelism with silence. They are not altering the gospel, but asserting that there is no gospel. 'We have nothing to say,' they affirm. 'Our calling is to sit down alongside secular man and let him teach us. We cannot aspire to be more than a Christian presence in the midst of the non-Christian world.'[4] But this is to abandon evangelism altogether. The need to penetrate into non-Christian society is agreed, but what

[3] p. 17.
[4] For example, 'the calling of the church to be the missionary presence of Christ in such a way as to reveal to the world God's redeeming presence'. Again, 'a missionary congregation, like a band of missionaries, fulfils its calling by being present as a servant people among men'. (See *Planning for Mission*, pp. 122 and 220.)

is needed is penetration with a view to proclamation, not silence. Nothing to say? When did the gospel cease to be 'good news' and the Church cease to be the 'herald' God has appointed to announce it?

Yet others seem, if I may put it thus, to escape from the call to evangelize by plunging into good works of healing, education and social reform. These are right and necessary. Yet the final and universal commission of Christ, recorded at the end of the gospels, was neither to heal the sick (as it had been when He sent out the twelve and the seventy), nor to reform society, but to preach the gospel. What then is the place of social action? And what is its relation to evangelism? Social action is not to be equated with evangelism, nor is it a constituent part of evangelism, nor is it primarily a means to evangelism (hospital patients and school pupils being a conveniently captive audience for the gospel). Like evangelism, social action must stand on its own feet and in its own right: both are the services of love, a part of the *diakonia* of Christ and of Christians, as He calls them to follow in His footsteps. Nevertheless, although they must not be identified with one another, they should not be isolated from one another either. The two walk together hand in hand, neither pretending to be the other, nor using the other as its cloak or prop.

The Church is committed, then, to preach the gospel to the world, and the gospel is 'eternal'[5] and 'imperishable'.[6] What is it? Paul called it 'the gospel of God'.[7] The genitive could be objective, so that the gospel is good news about God, His nature and purposes. And so it is,

[5] Rev. 14:6.
[6] 'the sacred and imperishable proclamation of eternal salvation'— a phrase from the so-called Shorter Ending of Mark.
[7] Rom. 1:1.

to some extent. Jesus spoke of 'the gospel of the kingdom of God', the good news that through the Messiah He was now establishing His rule in the lives of men.[8] Paul also referred to 'the gospel of the grace of God' and linked it with 'heralding the kingdom'.[9]

THE PERSON OF CHRIST

All this is true. But at the beginning of Paul's letter to the Romans, where he uses the expression 'the gospel of God', it is plain that God is the subject not the object of the genitive. It is God who conceived, engineered and published the gospel, whereas the substance of the good news is Christ: 'Paul . . . called to be an apostle, set apart for the gospel of God . . . concerning his Son . . . Jesus Christ our Lord'.[10] The gospel of God concerns the Son of God; it is an announcement about Christ. The Holy Spirit bears witness 'concerning' Christ,[11] and the apostolic message could be summarized in the words 'him we proclaim'.[12]

The central truth of the good news, then, is Christ Himself. This immediately raises a question. If we are called to preach the gospel, and the gospel is about Christ, where are we to get our information about Christ? Put differently, if we are to preach Christ, which Christ are we to preach? To these questions we must reply: we are not to preach a vague Christ, but a precise and particular Christ, namely the Christ of the New Testament. There is no other Christ to preach. Indeed, our knowledge of

[8] For example, Luke 4:43; Matt. 24:14. Cf. Mark 1:14 f.
[9] Acts 20:24 f.
[10] Rom. 1:1-4. Cf. Mark 1:1.
[11] John 15:26. Cf. Acts 1:8.
[12] Col. 1:28.

Christ is almost entirely limited to what the apostolic eye-witnesses tell us about Him. Christ chose and appointed them to bear witness to Him, because they had been with Him from the beginning.[13] Their witness is primary, and permanently normative; our witness must be subordinate to and regulated by theirs. If Christ Himself was unique, the Word made flesh, then the apostles' witness to Christ was equally unique. Their teaching about Him can no more be altered or superseded than can Christ Himself. It is and always will be 'through their word' alone that men come to believe in Him.[14]

What is it about the apostles' Christ which constitutes good news? Whether we read the gospels, the Acts sermons, or the New Testament epistles, there can be no doubt that the foundation of the gospel is the historical fact of Christ, His birth, life, death, resurrection, ascension and gift of the Spirit. These are successive links of the one chain. They are all aspects of the inclusive fact that He 'came' or 'was sent' into the world.

The apostles do not present these events as mere historical facts, however, but as meaningful facts, purposive events, distinctive parts of the saving action of God. The very first proclamation of the good news was the angelic announcement on Christmas Day: 'I bring you good news of a great joy . . . for to you is born this day in the city of David a Saviour, who is Christ the Lord'.[15] Such was the significance of His given name, 'Jesus'.[16] The apostles enforce this. 'The Father sent the Son to be

---

[13] John 15:27. Cf. Acts 1:21 f.
[14] John 17:20.
[15] Luke 2:10 f.
[16] Matt. 1:21.

the Saviour of the world', wrote John.[17] And Paul's summary was that 'Christ Jesus came into the world to save sinners'.[18]

So the gospel is about Christ, who came to save us. And His salvation is a comprehensive deliverance from all sin. It begins with our forgiveness and our reconciliation to God. It continues with our progressive liberation from the downdrag of indwelling sin and with our transformation into the image of Christ. It will be consummated at Christ's return when we are given new bodies in a new world, from which all sin has been for ever excluded.

It is tragic beyond words that this high and holy purpose of God to save men through Christ has been frequently diluted by the Church. Instead of the faithful proclamation of this good news, evangelism becomes a pathetic exhortation to bad men to be good and (more often) supposedly good men to be better, or an attempt to induce people to come to church and worship, or to apply Christian principles to industry, or even to find the highest common factor between Christian 'faith' and non-Christian 'faiths' so that we may minimize our differences and join in corporate devotion.

THE DEATH OF CHRIST

If we now ask what Christ did to secure salvation for sinners, the chief answer is: 'He died.' Although every event of His earthly visit is part of His saving career, He actually achieved our salvation in and by His death. He also showed its centrality in His own mind by instituting the Supper which commemorates it. So plain is this in the

[17] I John 4:14.
[18] I Tim. 1:15.

New Testament that it would not need demonstration, were it not that it is constantly denied. Phrases like 'Christ died for our sins', 'Christ gave himself for our sins', 'Christ having been offered once to bear the sins of many', 'Christ also died for sins once for all'[19] occur so often that they should be impossible to miss. It is never written in Scripture that He 'lived for our sins' or 'rose for our sins'. His work for our sins is always associated with His death. What cleanses us from sin is His 'blood', the virtue of His sacrificial death, and that alone.[20] Important as are His birth and resurrection, His supernatural entry into and exit from this life, they are viewed in Scripture in relation to His death. His birth prepared for His death and His resurrection confirmed its saving efficacy. In I Timothy 2:5, 6 Christ Jesus is given three separate titles: 'mediator', 'man', and 'ransom'. A careful study of the passage reveals that His ransom-paying death is pivotal. He became man in order to become a ransom, and because He gave Himself as a ransom once He can be our mediator today. Without this central act of blood-shedding as the ransom price for sin, His manhood would be largely purposeless and His mediation entirely impossible.

What then did Christ do? We must be loyal to the apostles' teaching. The effect of Christ's death is not only upon sin (to put it away), upon the devil (to deprive him of power) and upon us (to redeem and inspire us), but upon God Himself. Of course the whole saving movement began with God as well as ending with Him. But what God initiated and completed through Christ was a deliberate action to enable Him justly to turn judgment into justification.

[19] I Cor. 15:3; Gal. 1:4; Heb. 9:28; I Pet. 3:18.
[20] For example, Eph. 1:7; Heb. 9:22; I John 1:7.

We ask again: what did Christ do? He died. To say this is not simply to state a fact, but to explain it, because human death in Scripture is never a meaningless phenomenon. On the contrary, death is always a fact of theological significance, the dreadful penalty for human sin. From the second chapter of Genesis ('in the day that you eat of it you shall die') to the penultimate chapter of Revelation (in which impenitent sinners die 'the second death') the same theme is consistently emphasized: 'the wages of sin is death'.[21] Since Jesus had no sin either in His nature or in His conduct, He need never have died, either physically or spiritually. He could have been 'translated' like Enoch and Elijah. He nearly was—at the Transfiguration. But He deliberately stepped back into this world, in order voluntarily to lay down His life. Then why did He do it? What was the rationale of His death? There is only one possible, logical, biblical answer. It is that He died for *our* sins, not His own. The death He died was our death, the penalty which our sins had richly deserved. For these sins He died, not only in body but in soul, in the awful God-forsaken darkness. The evidence for this is not simply in isolated proof texts but in the whole scriptural witness to the relation between sin and death.

Our evangelistic duty is now clear. We are to 'preach Christ crucified'.[22] And so vivid is our proclamation to be, that we must portray Christ crucified before people's eyes, as if placarding Him on a public billboard.[23] We are also to make it plain that Christ's cross is the only ground on which God can accept sinners.

[21] Gen. 2:17; Rev. 21:8; Rom. 6:23.
[22] I Cor. 1:23.
[23] Gal. 3:1.

This 'word of the cross'[24] has always been unpopular. In Paul's own day it was 'a stumbling block to Jews and folly to Gentiles'.[25] That is, it was offensive both to Jewish self-righteousness and to Greek intellectualism. In effect, it asserted that Jews could not make their own way to God by their morality, nor Greeks by their philosophy. If they would humble themselves before the cross, however, they would find it to be the wisdom and the power of God.[26]

The 'stumbling block of the cross'[27] remains. Sinners hate it because it tells them that they cannot save themselves. Preachers are tempted to avoid it because of its offensiveness to the proud. It is easier to preach man's merits than Christ's, because men greatly prefer it that way. So we are presented with the alternative of 'preaching Christ crucified' or 'preaching circumcision'.[28] To preach circumcision is to proclaim man's ability to save himself by his own obedience; to preach Christ crucified is to proclaim Christ as the one and only Saviour.

I fear that many of us yield to the temptation to avoid the scandal of the cross. We 'preach circumcision', appealing to the powers and prowess of men. And we do it for the same reason as the Judaizers did: 'only in order that they may not be persecuted for the cross of Christ'.[29] Paul himself had felt the insidious power of this temptation. Otherwise he would never have written: 'I decided [it was a deliberate resolve, you see] to know nothing among you except Jesus Christ and him crucified.'[30] In the face of

[24] I Cor. 1:18.
[25] I Cor. 1:23.
[26] I Cor. 1:24.
[27] Gal. 5:11.
[28] Gal. 5:11.
[29] Gal. 6:12.
[30] I Cor. 2:2.

growing contemporary opposition to the apostolic gospel of Christ crucified, we need the same stern determination today.

One man who followed in the footsteps of Paul, even against the fierce opposition of men, was Charles Simeon, Dean of King's College and vicar of Holy Trinity, Cambridge, at the beginning of the nineteenth century. A tablet on the south wall of the church commemorates him as one 'who, whether as the ground of his own hopes or as the subject of all his ministrations determined to know nothing but Jesus Christ and Him crucified . . .'

THE BIBLE VIEW OF MAN

If the gospel of God concerns Christ crucified as the Saviour of sinners, this tells us something about man as well as about Christ. Indeed, the New Testament gospel of Christ presupposes the biblical doctrine of sin, and much attempted evangelism is undermined from the start because this doctrine is rejected. The gospel is good news from God, about Christ, to man. Who is this man to whom the gospel is addressed?

The Bible never forgets man's dignity. Although fallen, he is still 'made in the likeness of God'.[31] Moreover, Christ died for him, which shows what his worth is to God. It also shows the gravity of his plight, since nothing less than the death of God's Son could have secured his redemption.

But the fact about man which the Bible is most concerned to emphasize is that he is a sinner, and that his sin has at least three grave consequences. First, he is under the judgment of God. Sin is a revolt against the authority of God and a bid for independence. It therefore brings us

[31] Jas. 3:9.

37

under God's judgment, God's wrath. Man is, in fact, the object of God's love and wrath concurrently. The God who condemns man for his disobedience has already planned how to justify him. Three verses in the first chapter of Romans summarize this. 'The gospel,' Paul writes, 'is the power of God for salvation . . . For in it the righteousness of God is revealed (that is, God's way of putting sinners right with Himself) . . . For the wrath of God is revealed from heaven against all ungodliness and wickedness . . .'[32] Precisely how God's wrath is being revealed from heaven against sin is not explained; Paul is probably referring to the fearful process of moral deterioration which works in wilful sinners whom God gives up to their own wilfulness, and which he describes at the end of the chapter. But if God's wrath is seen in the corruption of man and of society, His remedy for sin is seen in the gospel. There are thus two revelations of God. His righteousness (or way of salvation) is revealed in the gospel, because His wrath is revealed from heaven against all unrighteousness. So the God of the Bible is a God of love and wrath, of mercy and judgment. And all the restlessness, pleasure-seeking and escapism that mark the life of man in every age, and all the world over, are symptomatic of his judicial estrangement from God.

In addition to being under the judgment of God, man is in bondage to his own selfish nature. 'Every one who commits sin is a slave to sin,' Jesus said,[33] and Paul constantly alludes to this slavery.[34]

Thirdly, man is helpless to save himself either from

[32] Rom. 1:16-18.
[33] John 8:34.
[34] For example, Rom. 6:15-23; Eph. 2:1-3; Titus 3:3.

judgment or from bondage. He cannot merit God's favour and he cannot secure his own release. He is in both senses the prisoner of sin. Only the free grace of God in Christ can reach and rescue him.

This truth, and the language in which it is expressed, are calculated to raise many hackles. It is commonly said that the gospel can no longer be presented in these terms. Two chief objections are lodged.

First, we are being assured that man has now attained his majority, and that 'man come of age' has no need of the old-fashioned God of the Bible or of the outmoded salvation which He offers. This concept of man's maturity was not invented by the Bishop of Woolwich. R. Gregor Smith expounded it in *The New Man*[35] and traced its origins to the Renaissance. Dietrich Bonhoeffer had paved the way during the war in his *Letters and Papers from Prison*:[36] 'Man has learned to cope with all questions of importance without recourse to God as a working hypothesis.'[37] Indeed, God Himself 'is teaching us that we must live as men who can get along very well without Him . . .'[38]

But there is a fundamental confusion here. It is true that the Renaissance and the Industrial Revolution, burgeoning into the achievements of modern technology, have created a man so different from his pre-scientific ancestors as to seem 'new' and 'mature' indeed. He wields power and authority of which his forebears never even dreamed. He is able to control his environment, and bend the forces of nature to his own will. Further, in doing so, he is fulfilling

[35] S.C.M. Press, 1956.
[36] S.C.M. Press, 1953.
[37] p. 145.
[38] p. 164.

God's creation command to 'fill the earth and subdue it'.[39] But he is not a new man morally or spiritually. In this, far from coming of age, he is but a child. He must therefore humble himself like a little child, as Jesus said, if he is ever to 'enter' or 'receive' God's kingdom.[40]

The God of the biblical Christian has sometimes been termed the 'God of the gaps' because it is supposed that we resort to Him only when we cannot fill the *lacunae* in our knowledge. Now that scientific discovery is steadily reducing the number of these gaps, the argument runs, God is being squeezed out. One day there will be no gaps left, and we shall then be able to dispense with Him altogether. Long before the current fashion of the 'death of God' theology had been thought of, this notion had been expressed. In a manifesto adopted by the Secularist League at Liège in 1865 it was said: 'science has made God unnecessary.'[41]

What is utterly bogus about this confident claim to have closed the gaps and dispensed with God is that at least two gaps are as wide as ever and will never be filled by human ingenuity. The first is the gulf between God and man caused by man's sin and God's judgment upon it, and the second is the gulf between man as he is and man as God meant him to be. Technology cannot span these gaps, nor can secular education teach us to build our own bridges. Only God can cross this great divide. And He has taken the initiative in Christ to do so.

So *this* is what the gospel is about. 'Man come of age' in a technological world is still man in sin and under judgment, man the slave of his passions and helpless to save himself.

[39] Gen. 1:28.
[40] For example, Mark 10:13-16; Matt. 18:1-4.
[41] *Towards the Conversion of England*, p. 9.

Contrary to what is often asserted nowadays, many people are still aware of this their human predicament. Let me give you an example. A friend of mine during the Second World War was the Sub-Lieutenant serving as navigator on the destroyer H.M.S. *Eclipse*. He tells me that he could not escape from four realities. First, he made great resolves to break free from sin, only to be humiliated by repeated failure. Secondly, he knew he had broken God's laws. It used to strike him that if the 'King's Regulations and Admiralty Instructions' were held in great honour, with various unalterable penalties, God must be at least as just as the King and the Lords of the Admiralty. Thirdly, his sense of accountability to God increased when he was on watch by himself and remembered the unwelcome fact that death was possibly very near. Fourthly, his sense of sin and need was heightened by the awe-inspiring sights of the creation. 'If the God with whom I had to do had made the vast Atlantic rollers which carried us up and down with such irresistible power, then how great was He against whom I knew I had sinned. On watch at night the serenity and eternity of the stars also spoke of this same indescribably powerful God.' Yet during this period he took pains to hide his guilty fears 'beneath a cloak of gaiety and fun'. At that time he never knew, nor even imagined, he says, that 'God Himself stooped to meet my desperate need on the cross. Words fail to praise the Lord Jesus for all He has done!'

I could echo much of this from my own experience. What brought me to Christ was a sense of defeat and of estrangement, and the astonishing news that the historic Christ offered to meet the very needs of which I was conscious.

Here is another example, this time from a non-Christian country. I have heard Dr. Chandu Ray, Bishop of Karachi, tell of a visit he once paid to a college in Pakistan, where most of the students were Muslims. When he offered personal interviews, a hundred and twenty-one responded. But they did not want to talk with him about theology, about Islam and Christianity, or about the Trinity. Their great question was: 'Is there a way of release from our soiled conscience which torments us?'

THE SENSE OF SIN

The results of the questionnaire submitted to members of our church in London confirm this. Some admitted that what led them to Christ was a sense not so much of sin as that 'life was a great burden and pointless' or 'purposeless', or that they felt 'unloved and unwanted'. But, in answer to the question 'At the time of your conversion what was your understanding of sin and guilt?', seventy-five out of one hundred and five claimed to have been fairly clear. A significant number were explicit. Here are a few examples: 'I was fully aware that I was leading a corrupt life.' 'I knew I was guilty before God.' 'I was fully conscious of my sin and guilt . . . I wept over them.' 'I had an acute sense of sin that sometimes led me to despair.' 'I hated my own shortcomings which drove me to Christ.'

So we must insist that the emergence of a so-called 'new man', scientifically speaking, does not alter the gospel. Underneath he is still the old man. Just as there was no distinction between Jew and Greek, since all are sinners who fall short of God's glory,[42] so today there is no

[42] Rom. 3:22 f.

distinction between Hindu and Muslim, Buddhist and pagan, technological man and primitive man. The gospel is addressed to men as men, sinful men, suffering the disastrous ill effects of the same fall, inheriting the same warped nature (however much their temperaments may vary), condemned under the same judgment and imprisoned in the same bondage.

This brings us to the second objection. Supposing we accept the biblical estimate of man outlined above, the problem is that man does not know himself. If he were to read the Bible, he would not recognize his own portrait. Besides, we are often told, he is neither troubled about sin nor interested in salvation. Therefore, our critics continue, it is futile using these categories when you talk to him, *however true they may be*. You put yourself into the ludicrous position of answering questions which he is not asking.

There are two possible reactions to this situation. The first is to give in to it. What we must do in this case, since modern men are not enquiring how to be saved, is to discover what questions they are asking. Then we shall be in a position to answer (or attempt to answer) not the questions which we think they ought to be asking, but the questions which they are in fact asking.

Now, of course, there is an important truth here. We must take people as we find them and speak in terms of their experience. If Jesus could use wind and water to introduce and enforce spiritual truths with Nicodemus and the Samaritan woman, we must follow His example. More than that, He stressed with them that aspect of the gospel which suited their need. We too must be alert to the felt needs of modern men—frustration, boredom, fear, loneliness, and meaninglessness. We must beware of giving them inept treatment like the enthusiast who is said to have applied vigorous artificial respiration to an unconscious person who was later found to have broken a rib!

But are we to stop with a person's felt need? If he is lonely, are we content to speak to him only of Jesus the Friend, or, if frustrated, about the sense of purpose which Jesus gives? Are we to acquiesce in a situation in which people are not asking the right questions? If we did so, we would have to give up preaching the gospel altogether. We would become blind leaders of the blind. We would resemble a doctor who listens carefully to a patient's own account of his illness, accepts it, and proceeds at once to treat it, without ever bothering to examine him and make an independent diagnosis. This is the most irresponsible thing a doctor could do. It is tantamount to allowing the patient to be his own doctor. No. The doctor's job is not to accept the patient's view of his trouble, but, after both listening to him and examining him, to reach his own opinion. Then he will decide on the treatment, help the patient to understand why it is necessary, and so induce him to co-operate.

The anology is not perfect, but it is exact enough for our purpose. Men and women are sick, sin-sick. Many of them do not know it. Before they are willing to take the medicine of the gospel, they must learn the truth about themselves and come to believe it. If we weakly acquiesce in their self-diagnosis, we shall be bad physicians who deserve to be struck off the register. We shall resemble the prophets and priests of Judah, of whom God said: 'They have healed the wound of my people lightly, saying "Peace, peace," when there is no peace'.[43]

[43] Jer. 6:14.

It is remarkable how, in New Testament days, people seemed to be asking the right questions. The rich young ruler came running to Jesus with this query: 'What must I do to inherit eternal life?'[44] The crowd who heard Peter on the Day of Pentecost were 'cut to the heart' and cried out: 'Brethren, what shall we do?'[45] And the Philippian jailor rushed into the cell where Paul and Silas were, fell down before them trembling with fear, and asked: 'Men, what must I do to be saved?'[46] Would that men and women asked such straight questions more frequently today! Only the Holy Spirit can cause them to do so. How this happens, and the means He employs to bring conviction of sin, I must leave to the last chapter. Meanwhile it is enough for me to say that, if we stop short of the subjects of sin and salvation, or eliminate them from our message, we betray the gospel. The seventeenth-century Jesuits in China, in order not to upset the social sensitivities of the Chinese, excluded the crucifixion and certain other details from the gospel. But, Professor Hugh Trevor-Roper has written, 'we do not learn that they made many lasting converts by the unobjectionable residue of the story'.[47]

If then we refuse to truncate the gospel, and insist on retaining in our proclamation of it the basic themes of sin and salvation, does this mean that we can never go on to the latter until conviction of the former has dawned? No. Two further points must be made before we leave this subject. First, as a matter of experience, many are converted without any clear understanding or sense of their

[44] Mark 10:17.
[45] Acts 2:37.
[46] Acts 16:30.
[47] In a letter to *The Times* on December 1st, 1959.

sin and guilt. I mention this as a fact to be noted, not as a warrant to eliminate sin from our presentation of the gospel.

Secondly, Scripture teaches and experience confirms that a sense of sin's gravity often comes upon people after their new birth, rather than before it. 'A new heart I will give you, and a new spirit I will put within you . . . And I will deliver you from all your uncleannesses . . . Then you will remember your evil ways, and your deeds that were not good; and you will loathe yourselves for your iniquities and your abominable deeds.'[48]

THE RESPONSE OF FAITH

So far, in our consideration of the gospel of God, we have concentrated on Christ and man, on grace and sin. The third element to be added is man's response to Christ. For, although Christ finished His work on the cross, He does not impose His salvation upon men willy-nilly, nor do men automatically benefit from it. Every individual sinner must 'believe in' Christ crucified if he is to receive and enjoy 'the benefits of His passion'.

Faith is variously described and illustrated in the New Testament. Essentially it is a confiding trust. The fourth gospel is rich in teaching on the nature of faith. It equates 'believing in' (or into) Christ with 'coming to' Christ.[49] Both imply motion, a step of self-committal. And John records two of our Lord's most graphic illustrations. His conversation with Nicodemus appears to have ended with one: 'As Moses lifted up the serpent in the wilderness, so must the Son of man be lifted up, that

[48] Ezek. 36:26-31.
[49] For example, 6:35; 7:37 f.

whoever believes in him may have eternal life.'[50] Here the poisonous snakebites which were proving fatal among the Israelites near Mount Hor are taken as a picture of man's spiritual condition, 'perishing' through his sin. And saving faith is looking to Christ crucified for eternal life, as the Israelites looked to the uplifted brazen serpent for healing.

The second illustration is in the discourse in John 6 about 'the bread of life'. In verse 47 Jesus says 'he who believes has eternal life', and in verse 54 'he who eats my flesh and drinks my blood has eternal life'. Since Christ's flesh is what He will 'give for the life of the world' (v. 51), and His blood is His life sacrificed or laid down, and since 'eating and drinking' are equated with 'believing', we must conclude that saving faith is a personal appropriation of Christ crucified.

What is striking about these two bold images is that in both of them the object of faith is the crucified Christ, lifted up on the cross and shedding His blood. Further, both analogies show that the value of faith is not at all in itself but entirely in its object. What saves men from perishing and brings them eternal life is not the eye of faith but the uplifted Christ who is gazed upon, not the mouth of faith but the sacrificed Christ whose flesh and blood are spiritually consumed. So the sole function of faith is to appropriate the Christ who once died and now offers Himself to us as our Saviour. Salvation is by the grace of Christ alone, through the faith of men alone.

What then about repentance and surrender? Although the call to repent was regularly sounded forth by the apostles when they preached the gospel, it is often muted today. Some evangelists go so far as to divorce the

[50] 3:14 f.

acceptance of Christ as Saviour from the submission to Christ as Lord, emphasizing the first at conversion and relegating the second to some later date. They even argue that to add repentance to faith, in gospel preaching, is to violate the principle of *sola fides*, 'faith alone', and to introduce 'works' by the back door.

This is not so. The summons to serve Christ as King is 'not an appendix to the evangel, but an integral part of it . . . Believing in Christ and obeying Him are not two acts, but two phases of one act. Trusting Christ as Saviour and acknowledging Him as Lord are inseparable. The latter is the acid test of the former'.[51] In his Corinthian correspondence Paul summarizes his evangelistic proclamation both as 'we preach Christ crucified'[52] and as 'we preach . . . Jesus Christ as Lord'.[53] The Christ we proclaim is one Christ, who died to be our Saviour and has been raised and exalted as Lord. It is utterly impossible to cut Him into pieces, to separate His saviourhood from His lordship, and then to respond to the one while ignoring the other. No, the object of saving faith is precisely 'the Lord Jesus Christ'.[54]

Hence the response to the gospel which the Christian evangelist desires is called the 'obedience of faith'.[55] The faith which apprehends Christ also surrenders to Christ. It asks no terms and makes no conditions. Repentance and surrender are not added to faith as supplements; rather,

---

[51] R. B. Kuiper: *God-Centred Evangelism*, pp. 169 f. It is not without significance, in this connection, that the passive form of the Greek verb *peithō* can be translated either 'be persuaded' and so 'believe' (e.g. Acts 17:4; 28:24) or 'obey' (e.g. Rom. 2:8; Gal. 5:7).
[52] I Cor. 1:23.
[53] II Cor. 4:5.
[54] Acts 16:31.
[55] Rom. 1:5; 16:26 (literally).

a true, living and saving faith is such a complete commitment to a complete Christ that it includes them. This is 'conversion'. Whether it is sudden or gradual, and what its relation is to regeneration and baptism, I leave to the last chapter.

Thus the gosepl we preach anticipates a new life for all who embrace it, a life lived under the yoke of Christ,[56] a life which begins at the foot of Christ's cross and continues as we take up our own cross daily and follow Him.[57]

If the desired response is 'obedience of faith', how is it elicited? It is certainly the work of the Holy Spirit, without whom 'no one can say "Jesus is Lord".'[58] Therefore there is a great danger in what is sometimes called 'decisionism', as if all a man has to do is to pull himself together, exercise his will power and 'decide for Christ'. *Towards the Conversion of England* sometimes falls into this way of speaking. It acknowledges that 'from first to last salvation is a downward act of intervention from God to man', and that even man's acceptance of salvation is due to the work of the Holy Spirit,[59] but then it spoils it by referring elsewhere to 'an appeal to decide for Christ'. The very language of 'decisions' and 'decision-cards', though doubtless of practical convenience, is too man-centred to be anything but gravely misleading. Article X (*Of Free-Will*) is more biblical in stating: 'The condition of man after the fall of Adam is such, that he cannot turn and prepare himself, by his own natural strength and good works, to faith and calling upon God.'

Does this mean that the evangelist can do nothing but

[56] Matt. 11:29.
[57] Luke 9:23.
[58] I Cor. 12:3.
[59] p. 145.

49

wait for God to work? No, indeed not, for how are men to 'believe in him of whom they have never heard? And how are they to hear without a preacher?'[60] The means God has chosen to elicit faith in unbelievers is the preaching of His own Word.[61] It is still through 'what we preach' that God saves those who believe.[62] We must therefore be faithful in expounding and explaining the gospel. We must go further than that. There is good biblical precedent for actually beseeching or begging men, in Christ's name, to be reconciled to God.[63] Indeed, if our proclamation does not issue in such an appeal, our gospel-preaching is bound to be lopsided.

We have seen that the three major constituents of the gospel of God are Jesus Christ and Him crucified, the plight and peril of man in sin and under judgment, and the necessary response called 'obedience of faith'. Or, in simple monosyllables, 'sin—grace—faith'. This is the irreducible minimum.

Is it not too theological? I have heard it said that we should 'seek to impart a minimum of truth' and point to Christ as the way 'without doctrinal formulation'. With this viewpoint the apostles would certainly have disagreed. Their presentation of the gospel was remarkably rich in intellectual content. They 'reasoned' with people out of the Scriptures, and sought to 'persuade' them of the truth of their message.[64] They therefore described conversion sometimes as a believing acknowledgment of the truth,[65] and even as an obedience to the form or 'standard of teach-

[60] Rom. 10:14.
[61] Rom. 10:17
[62] I Cor. 1:21.
[63] II Cor. 5:20.
[64] For example, Acts 17:2-4; 19:8-10.
[65] For example, II Thess. 2:10-12.

ing' to which the hearers had been committed.[66] As the Jerusalem Bible translates this last verse: 'you submitted without reservation to the creed you were taught.' We must therefore agree with *Towards the Conversion of England* that 'to "preach the gospel" means preaching Christian dogma.'[67]

[66] Rom. 6:17.
[67] p. 66.

CHAPTER THREE

THE CHURCH OF GOD

THE EVANGELISTIC AGENCY

We have considered the major reasons why evangelism is right and necessary, and the substance of the message to be proclaimed. Now who is to be the messenger?

The first and fundamental answer to this question is 'God Himself'. The gospel is God's gospel. He conceived it. He gave it its content. He publishes it. The fact that He has committed to us both 'the ministry of reconciliation' and 'the message of reconciliation'[1] does not alter this. He acted 'through Christ' to achieve the reconciliation and now acts 'through us' to announce it.[2] But He still remains Himself both reconciler and preacher.

He has used other and more exalted agencies through whom to publish salvation before partially delegating the work to the Church. Apart from Old Testament prophets, the first herald of the gospel was an angel, and the first announcement of it was accompanied by a display of the glory of the Lord and greeted by the worship of the heavenly host.[3]

Next, God sent His Son, who was Himself both the messenger and the message. For God sent a 'word . . . to Israel, preaching good news of peace by Jesus Christ'.[4]

[1] II Cor. 5:18, 19.
[2] II Cor. 5:18, 20.
[3] Luke 2:8-14.
[4] Acts 10:36.

So Jesus not only 'made peace' between God and man, Jew and Gentile, but also 'preached peace'.[5] He went about Palestine announcing the good news of the kingdom.

Next, God sent His Spirit to bear witness to Christ.[6] So the Father Himself witnesses to the Son through the Spirit. And only now does He give the Church a privileged share in the testimony: 'and you also will bear witness'.[7]

It is essential to remember these humbling truths. The chief evangelist is God the Father, and He proclaimed the evangel through His angel, His Son and His Spirit before He entrusted any part of the task to men. This was the order. The Church comes at the bottom of the list. And the Church's witness will always be subordinate to the Spirit's. It is less that we do the witnessing and He confirms our testimony, than that He bears the witness and we corroborate His.

Having said this, we must not minimize either the honour or the importance of the ministry which God has given us. The Father could easily draw people to Christ through the Spirit without any human co-operation whatever. But He has chosen normally not to do so. He has appointed His Church to be the herald of the gospel to the ends of the earth. Striking examples of God's use of human agents in evangelism are given us in Acts 8, 9 and 10. Here the curtain is lifted and we are permitted to see behind the scenes. We watch the invisible drama of conversion being enacted, with God at work in the experience of both enquirer and evangelist. In chapter 8 He guides Philip the evangelist to the chariot of a seeking Ethiopian

[5] Eph. 2:14-17; Col. 1:20.
[6] John 15:26.
[7] John 15:27 (literally).

eunuch. In chapter 9 Saul of Tarsus, having been 'appre-
hended' by Christ Jesus without human agency outside
the Damascus gates, is welcomed into the Church by
Ananias. In chapter 10 God directs the Roman centurion
Cornelius to send a deputation to Peter, and meanwhile
directs Peter to go back with them to Caesarea.

The evangelistic agency God employs then is His people,
the Church. There is no more forceful statement of this
truth in the New Testament than that given by the Apostle
Peter in the second chapter of his first epistle. He calls the
Church 'a chosen race, a royal priesthood, a holy nation,
God's own people'.[8] But he did not invent these epithets.
He borrowed them from Exodus 19, verses 5 and 6, where
through Moses God had applied them to the redeemed
Israelites, with whom He was about to establish His
covenant. Led by the Holy Spirit Peter boldly reapplies
them to God's new Israel, the Church. For it is the Church
of Christ today which occupies the unique position as the
chosen people of God which was formerly held by Israel
according to the flesh.

But why has God chosen His people to be this royal,
priestly, holy, special community? It is not mainly for
their own benefit. Their election is for God and for the
world. So their first duty as God's redeemed people is
worship: 'to offer spiritual sacrifices acceptable to God
through Jesus Christ' (v. 5); and their second duty is
witness: 'that you may declare the wonderful deeds of Him
who called you out of darkness into his marvellous light'
(v. 9).

It is not true therefore to say that the paramount
function of the Church is evangelism. God chose and

[8] Verse 9. Cf. verse 5.

54

called His people for Himself, to serve and glorify Him, for this is His due and their duty. But it is not His purpose that the Church should be an entirely inward and upward looking coterie, indifferent to the world outside. The vocation of the Church is to be occupied with God and with the world. God has constituted His Church to be a worshipping and witnessing community.

The ideal is noble and beautiful. But what is the practical reality to be? When we come down to brass tacks, what does it mean to say that evangelistic witness is the function of the whole Church? Precisely who is to do the witnessing? And how?

THE WORK OF AN EVANGELIST

Our first answer to this question must be that from the beginning Christ has appointed and endowed certain 'evangelists' with a particular gift and office of 'evangelism'. The word *evangelist* occurs in the New Testament only three times. When Paul applied it to Timothy he seems to have been referring to a part of Timothy's regular ministry and not to a particular *charisma*: 'do the work of an evangelist, fulfil your ministry'.[9] But the other two occurrences allude to a special appointment and gift. Jesus Christ, as Head of the Church, apportions different functions to different members of His body: 'his gifts were that some should be apostles, some prophets, some evangelists, some pastors and teachers'.[10] Only one such is mentioned by name in the New Testament, namely 'Philip the evangelist, who was one of the seven',[11] and

[9] II Tim. 4:5.
[10] Eph. 4:11.
[11] Acts 21:8.

who had given evidence of his gift when evangelizing Samaria and the Ethiopian Queen Candace's minister of state.[12]

There seems no reason to doubt that Christ can and does still give this evangelistic gift. Although the whole Church and every Church member are called to engage in the work of evangelism, there are some whom He specially appoints and equips as 'evangelists'. Such are endowed with an unusual ability to make the gospel plain and to lead people to embrace it.

The Anglican Communion scarcely seems to believe this today. One knows of gifted evangelists in England and elsewhere who, because the Church gives them no official recognition or financial support, are obliged to launch out on their own. One knows others who, after courageously continuing for some years in this exacting ministry, have been compelled because of family responsibilities to exchange their precarious livelihood for a more settled ministry. Is not this a scandal and a disgrace ? If Christ is still bestowing upon some 'the gift of an evangelist' and calling them to exercise their gift, the Church should be alert to recognize the gift, acknowledge the call, and set such men aside, free of monetary anxiety, to give themselves to this ministry. Are we so inflexibly tied to a concept of ministry embracing only the parochial system and certain institutional chaplaincies that we can make no room for the gifted foot-loose evangelist ?

Mention must also be made of evangelists with an international and interdenominational ministry, notably in our day Dr. Billy Graham. We thank God for him, and for raising him up to recall the Church in many places to

[12] Acts 8:4 ff and 26 ff.

its evangelistic task. We acknowledge that there is a place for 'mass evangelism' in special and occasional crusades, and that God has used them to the true and lasting conversion of large numbers of people. At the same time such campaigns are fraught with danger, of which Dr. Graham for one is keenly aware. Powerful psychological forces are at work in all mass meetings, and the temptation is strong to rely on these and on the organization itself for results, instead of on the Spirit of God. Missions may also isolate people from their home, work and church. Converted out of their *milieu*, they find it hard to become integrated again. Then there is the tendency of some campaigns to reap without regard to the sowing, and to bring to birth without concern for the baby's nurture. Again, all so-called 'missions', because sporadic in character and professional in leadership, can actually discourage genuine 'mission', which is the non-stop responsibility of non-professionals.

Of this too Billy Graham is convinced. I heard him say at a conference on evangelism convened by Dr. John Mackay at Princeton Theological Seminary in December 1956: 'If all churches were engaged in perennial evangelism, I don't think there would ever be need for a person like me.' In saying this, I think he somewhat overstated the case, for Christ does appoint 'evangelists' and there is room for special evangelistic missions. But these are to supplement the Church's regular mission, and fan it into flame, not to dampen it, still less to quench it altogether.

CHRIST'S WITNESSES

From particular 'evangelists' we now turn to the generality of 'witnesses'. This seems to be the best word to use. If

God does not call everyone to be an 'evangelist', He does not call everyone to be a 'minister', 'missionary' or 'preacher' either. But every Christian is a witness, and every Christian is called to bear witness.

We do not derive this fact from one of the commonest Scriptures quoted to prove it, however: 'Always be prepared to make a defence [A.V. 'to give an answer'] to any one who calls you to account for the hope that is in you'.[13] For this is a passive, defensive kind of witness, in which we speak only when we are spoken to, and explain our Christian hope only when we are challenged about it.

Christ expects His witnesses to take the initiative. 'You shall receive power when the Holy Spirit has come upon you; and you shall be my witnesses . . .' He said.[14] This is the risen Lord's standing order to all His followers. We can no more restrict the command to witness than we can restrict the promise of the Spirit. Not that the Christian witness has any warrant to be brash, indiscreet or discourteous. His witness is to be spontaneous and refreshing, the natural outflow of an interior spring.[15]

Such testimony is expected of every believer. We cannot keep the gospel to ourselves. It has been committed to us for others. We are stewards of it. We hold it in trust for the world. One of the plainest indications in Paul's epistles that every believer is required to be a witness is a statement in his Philippian letter. If his readers do not shine like stars in the night sky, he writes, if they do not hold forth the word of life, like waiters serving out some dainty dish, then he would regard all his Christian race

[13] I Pet. 3:15.
[14] Acts 1:8.
[15] Cf. John 4:14; 7:37-39.

58

and labour as having been in vain.[16] He was satisfied neither with their conversion, nor with their sanctification; they must be actively involved in evangelism as well.

The contemporary Church seems increasingly to recognize that the kind of 'every member canvass' which the Bible envisages is in reality an 'every member witness'. Bishop Azariah, of the diocese of Dornakal in South India, used to invite the newly baptized to place their hand on their head and say after him: 'I am a baptized Christian; woe is unto me if I preach not the gospel!'[17] And the Latin America Mission has for a number of years been promoting 'Evangelism-in-depth', a programme which involves the recruitment and training of whole churches over long periods.

William Temple's well-known words are quoted in *Towards the Conversion of England*: 'The evangelization of England . . . is a work that cannot be done by the clergy alone; it can only be done to a very small extent by the clergy at all. There can be no widespread evangelization of England, unless the work is undertaken by the lay people of the Church . . .'[18] The report took up this theme with enthusiasm. Its third chapter is entitled 'The Apostolate of the Whole Church', and it prints in bold type the statement: 'The ministry of evangelism is a charge laid upon the whole Church by its Lord. It is the very essence of the Christian calling.'[19]

The Lambeth Conference reports of 1948 and 1958 both contained some notable declarations of a similar kind. The bishops' encyclical letter in 1948 affirmed that 'the

[16] Phil. 2:15 f.
[17] Cf. I Cor. 9:16.
[18] p. 36.
[19] p. 40.

supreme task of the Church today is . . . to take the good news to those who have not heard it.' It continued: 'We call on all our people to engage in this campaign and to put themselves into training for it. Every man, woman and child has his part to take.'[20] The equivalent encyclical letter in 1958 affirmed that 'the world-wide task of evangelism is not an "optional extra": it is the high calling of every disciple.'[21] We suspect that Bishop Joost de Blank contributed the expression in inverted commas, because he had used it four years previously in his book *The Parish in Action*: 'Evangelism *is* the normal life of the Church, and can never be an optional extra.'[22] It is even possible that Bishop de Blank was borrowing from Abbé Michonneau, who wrote that the laity's 'apostolate is an essential part of their Christianity, and not "something extra".'[23]

Three further quotations from the 1958 Lambeth Conference report may be given: 'Evangelism is not to be thought of as the task of a select few . . . It is for every Christian to do what Andrew did for his brother—to say "we have found the Messiah" and to bring him to Jesus'.[24] Again, 'the work of evangelism is the duty and privilege of every member of Christ'.[25] Again, the task 'cannot be relegated to the specialist, to the "professional missionary" . . . The mission of the Church cannot mean less than *the whole Church bringing the whole gospel to the whole world*. To think of missionary activity (whether to the islands of the far seas or to the unevangelized masses of Great Britain or America) as a kind of "optional extra" to

[20] Part I, p. 17.
[21] p. 1.25.
[22] p. 17.
[23] p. 100.
[24] p. 2.75.
[25] p. 2.64.

be undertaken by those who are enthusiastic for that kind of thing, is to make complete nonsense of the gospel . . .'[26]

If it be granted that evangelism is the responsibility of the whole Church and every member of it, the first essential is contact—close personal contact. The yeast cannot do its leavening work unless it is inserted in the dough. The salt cannot stop decay until it is rubbed into the meat. No lamp gives light to the house if it is hidden away under a bed.

IDENTIFICATION WITH THE WORLD

What Jesus taught by these metaphors He put beyond possibility of misunderstanding by making His own mission the prototype of ours: 'As thou didst send me into the world, so I have sent them into the world'. 'As the Father has sent me, even so I send you'.[27] This 'as-so' does more than state a fact; it supplies a pattern. 'Mission' involves the Church, the gospel and the world. Yet it is not the Church declaiming the gospel from the house-tops to a distant, deaf and heedless world; it is the Church going out into the world with the gospel, infiltrating the world, identifying itself with the world, in order to share the gospel with the world.

Of the Son's 'identification' with the world into which He was sent, there can be no shadow of doubt. He did not remain in heaven; He came into the world. The word was not spoken from the sky; 'the Word was made flesh'. And then He 'dwelt among us'. He did not come on a fleeting visit and hurry back home again. He stayed in the world into which He came. He gave men a chance to behold His

[26] p. 2.66.
[27] John 17:18; 20:21.

glory. Nor did He only let them gaze from a distance. He scandalized the church leaders of His day by mixing with the riff-raff they avoided. 'Friend of publicans and sinners', they dubbed Him. To them it was a term of opprobrium; to us it is a title of honour. He touched untouchable lepers. He did not recoil from the caresses of a prostitute. And then He, who at His birth had been 'made flesh', was in His death 'made sin' and 'made a curse'.[28] He had assumed our nature; He now assumed our transgressions, our doom, our death. His self-identification with man was utter and complete.

Therefore when He says to us 'go', this is what He means. 'As our Lord took on our flesh, so he calls his Church to take on the secular world'; otherwise we do not 'take the Incarnation seriously'.[29] We are to go as He went, to penetrate human society, to mix with unbelievers and fraternize with sinners. Does not one of the Church's greatest failures lie here? We have disengaged too much. We have become a withdrawn community. We have been aloof, instead of alongside. Major W. Batt satirizes much of our evangelical practice as 'rabbit-hole Christianity'. He pictures a prim little Christian popping up from his Christian home each morning, like a rabbit out of its hole, making a brave little dash through the perilous outside world, and disappearing for safety into another burrow called 'my Christian office' for the rest of the day. Then, when work finishes, he summons up courage to emerge again, looking this way and that, only to bolt down a third hole called 'my Christian club'.

No doubt the caricature is overdrawn, as every carica-

[28] John 1:14; II Cor. 5:21; Gal. 3:13.
[29] *Witness in Six Continents*, pp. 151 and 158.

ture must be. But it is too accurate to be anything but painfully embarrassing, not only for those laity who enjoy a Christian insulation but for clergy too, whose whole training tends to cut them off from the people, at least from industrial, working people. If anyone doubts this, let him read Abbé Michonneau's outspoken chapter entitled *Clerical Culture*.[30]

Most people touch the world at three points at least—at work (if they are not employees of an exclusively Christian establishment), at home among neighbours, and in spare-time activities involving membership of sporting teams, social clubs, political activities and community service. We should welcome the contact with non-Christian people which all such opportunities bring. To go 'into the world' does not necessarily mean to travel to a distant country or primitive tribe. 'The world' is secular, godless society; it is all round us. Christ sends us 'into the world' when He puts us into any group which does not know or honour Him. It might be in our own street, or in an office or shop, school, hospital or factory, or even in our own family. And here in the world we are called to love, to serve and to offer genuine, sacrificial friendship. Paradoxically stated, the only truly Christian context in which to witness is the world.

Sometimes a Christian's connection with the world resembles that of a man-made satellite. He is in contact with it, but in orbit outside its atmosphere. And his entry into the world seems to him as difficult and dangerous as a satellite's re-entry. Indispensable as a genuine 'entry' is, it must not be misunderstood, however.

Let me enlarge on this. 'We believe,' wrote Simon

[30] *Revolution in a City Parish*, pp. 131-149.

Phipps, Coventry's Industrial Chaplain, explaining the work of the new cathedral consecrated in 1962, 'it is the Church's task to stand within the secular concerns of ordinary men and women, and with them to think out the deepest implications of these concerns . . . It is not a matter of shouting the gospel over the fence from outside, but of discovering it together from within.' To some extent this is well said, but the contrast is painted too starkly. We are certainly called to 'stand within the secular concerns' of ordinary people; but are the only alternatives 'shouting the gospel from outside' and 'discovering it together from within'? I do not believe the gospel is to be either 'shouted' or 'discovered'. Our commission is to 'herald' or 'proclaim' it, and in order to do so humbly, sympathetically and relevantly, we must first come sufficiently close to people to make shouting entirely unnecessary.

There are then two extremes to be avoided. The first is identification without proclamation, sitting alongside people with nothing to say, and with no intention of seeking to win them for Christ. We cannot surrender our God-given duty of proclamation. As David Winter has pertinently observed, in many places today 'the whole analogy of "fishing" is regarded as out-dated. Our Lord, it would seem, was quite wrong to tell Peter to be a fisherman and catch men. He should have told him to don a frogman's suit and try to identify himself with the fish!'[31]

Equally false is the opposite extreme of proclamation without identification, of offering pat solutions to problems we have never even attempted to understand. Douglas Webster, who likens the intellectual outsider to Job, also

[31] *Old Faith, Young World* (Hodder and Stoughton, 1965), p. 45.

likens some evangelists to Job's comforters 'with their easy words, their reasoned phrases, their glib dogmas and their safe distance from his existential situation'. He goes on: 'They were too ready to speak, too slow to listen. They never began to enter into Job's problem'. And later: 'If the Church is not itself to be misunderstood, then it must take infinite pains to understand'.[32]

Although modern radicals have gone much too far in their emphasis on identification without proclamation, learning without teaching, listening without speaking, we cannot help admiring both their missionary concern and their compassionate spirit. As the Archbishop of Canterbury has emphasized, we must 'go out and put ourselves with loving sympathy inside the doubts of the doubting, the questions of the questioners, and the loneliness of those who have lost their way'.[33]

Such an entry into men's hearts, born of compassion, is inevitably costly. We should not shrink from it on that account. The overseas missionary may give years to the gruelling task of mastering a foreign language; should we expect to learn without trouble the 'language' of other men's minds? As Canon John Taylor has put it, 'proclamation . . . involves a long-drawn-out effort to enter into the world of the other man'.[34]

HOLY WORLDLINESS

This brings us to the next point which needs to be made, namely that, indispensable as penetration is as a prelude to witness, it is no use the Church identifying with the

[32] *What is Evangelism?* pp. 58, 68.
[33] Michael Ramsey, Archbishop of Canterbury: *Images Old and New* (S.P.C.K., 1963), p. 14.
[34] *For All the World*, p. 34.

world if in doing so it ceases to be the Church. In a word, identification is not to be confused with assimilation. If the salt loses its saltness, it is useless. 'Men throw it away,' Jesus said.[35] It might just as well have stayed in the salt cellar. The disciple is not above his Master. Like Christ, therefore, the Christian is to be 'a friend of sinners' yet 'separated from sinners'.[36] We are to manifest a 'holy worldliness' (in Canon A. R. Vidler's famous phrase), because we are to be 'in the world' (worldly) and 'not of the world' (holy) at the same time.[37] We are called to live in natural surroundings a supernatural life, to demonstrate in this age the life of the age to come.

Certainly nothing hinders the progress of the gospel so much as our own inconsistent Christian lives. Too often we resemble the false teachers in Crete, of whom Paul wrote to Titus: 'They profess to know God, but they deny him by their deeds.'[38] Since we advance great claims for Christ, boasting that He saves His people from their sins, onlookers are perfectly justified when they demand to see in us some evidence to substantiate our claim to salvation.

As it is, we do not see ourselves as others see us. We do not realize how poor is our commendation of the Lord we love and seek to serve. More often than we know, what people reject is not the true Christ but the Christ they see in Christians—not Christ at all, in fact, but a rather unChristlike Church. Institutionalism, reactionary stuffiness, archaic liturgy, the establishment, absorption in the petty and the superficial—these are some of the features of modern religion, against which people revolt. 'If we

[35] Luke 14:34 f.
[36] Luke 7:34; Heb. 7:26.
[37] John 17:11-16.
[38] Titus 1:16.

Christians could put on Christ and put off "religion", we should be in a far better position for the evangelism of the outsider.'[39]

Towards the Conversion of England laid great stress on this need to commend the Saviour by an obviously 'saved' life: 'Ultimately the evidence for the credibility of the Gospel in the eyes of the world must be a quality of life manifested in the Church which the world cannot find elsewhere.'[40] Dean C. A. Alington of Durham took it up in a letter he wrote to *The Times* on January 28th, 1946: 'The best Christian evidence is that of Christian lives ... Good news, if it is believed, must eventually bear fruit in those "good works" which (more surely than argument) "put to silence the ignorance of foolish men".'

This need for the Church to be the Church and exhibit its true nature as a redeemed community is far more important than the adoption of any particular evangelistic techniques. This is how Dr. D. Martyn Lloyd-Jones, minister of Westminster Chapel in London, expresses it: 'We have been told that we have to make the Church attractive to the man outside, and the idea is to become as much like him as we can ...; yet ... the glory of the gospel is that when the Church is absolutely different from the world, she invariably attracts it ...' Again, 'Every revival proves clearly that men who are outside the Church always become attracted when the Church herself begins to function truly as the Christian Church, and as individual Christians approximate to the description here given in these Beatitudes.'[41]

This is true to experience. In the questionnaire sub-

[39] Douglas Webster: *What is Evangelism?*, p. 55.
[40] pp. 33 and 121.
[41] *Studies in the Sermon on the Mount* (I.V.F., 1959), vol. I, pp. 37, 54.

mitted to members of All Souls congregation I asked both: 'What first attracted you to Christ and the gospel?' and 'What mainly or finally brought you to Christ?' In their answers over half referred to something they had seen for themselves in Christian people, their parents, pastors, teachers, colleagues or friends. As one put it, these 'had something in their lives which I lacked but desperately longed for.' In several cases it was 'their external joy and inward peace'. To a student nurse it was 'the genuine and open friendship' offered by Christians; to an Oxford undergraduate studying law their 'sheer exuberance'; to a police constable the 'clear aim, purpose and idealism which Christian life offered' as seen in Christians; to a secretary in the B.B.C. 'the reality of the warmth and inner resources which I observed in Christians'; and to a house surgeon 'the knowledge of Christ's working in another person's life'.

To speak thus of outsiders being 'attracted' by the quality of Christian living does not necessarily mean, however, that Christians are always admired by non-Christians. On the contrary their lot is often to be rejected, not respected. Christ warned us that it would be so. He Himself, who was sent 'into the world' and lived 'in the world', yet because He was 'not of the world' was 'hated by the world'. These four expressions, all taken from John 15:18-25 and 17:11-18, sum up the reciprocal relations between Christ and the world. In the plainest possible terms Jesus added: 'If they persecuted me, they will persecute you'; and: 'If you were of the world, the world would love its own; but because you are not of the world, but I chose you out of the world, therefore the world hates you.'[42]

[42] John 15:20, 19.

Douglas Webster's exposition of this theme is succinct and moving. Let me quote a few phrases from it—'Mission sooner or later leads into passion. In biblical categories . . . the servant must suffer . . . Passion is not only the result but in some respects the climax of mission; it is that which makes mission effective . . . Every form of mission leads to some form of cross. The very shape of mission is cruciform. We can understand mission only in terms of the Cross . . .'[43]

THE LOCAL CHURCH

So far in this chapter we have been thinking of the evangelistic agency as either the special 'evangelist' or the individual 'witness'. Now we must consider the rôle of the local church. John saw the seven churches of Asia as 'seven lampstands';[44] and the purpose of a lampstand is to give to the light its maximum effectiveness. It is not only the individual Christian believer who is to let his light shine;[45] each local church is to be a lighthouse from which the bright beams of the gospel illumine the surrounding darkness. No church can evade its responsibility to be Christ's chosen instrument to bear His name and spread His message in the parish or neighbourhood in which it is situated. Some parishes are entirely inward looking; they need, as Bishop Joost de Blank found when he was vicar of Greenhill, Harrow, to be 'turned inside out'.[46]

Precisely how this could or should be done is receiving

[43] *Yes to Mission*, pp. 101 f. Cf. also *Local Church and World Mission*, pp. 47-49.
[44] Rev. 1:20.
[45] Matt. 5:14-16. Cf. Phil. 2:15.
[46] *The Parish in Action*, p. 88.

close attention in ecumenical circles, especially since a study on 'the missionary structure of the congregation' was authorized in 1961 at the Third Assembly of the World Council of Churches in New Delhi.[47] This quest for more flexible structures is of great importance for the Church's mission. But I can only write from experience of the more traditional pattern.

There are, of course, important differences between churches set in urban, suburban and rural districts. Nevertheless, the principles of local church evangelism are the same. Each church witnesses collectively in three main ways—by its fellowship, by its worship, and by its actual evangelistic outreach.

We begin with the fellowship of the church. What has been written above about the supernatural life of Christians is equally true of churches. Each local church, as a fellowship of redeemed sinners, God's own people, is a supernatural community. It betrays its true nature as a divine society only when it is characterized by divine love.

According to the questionnaire already mentioned, people are drawn to Christ not only by the example of individual Christians but by the corporate life of a Christian church. One person wrote of the effect of 'seeing a lot of Christians together' at a houseparty. Another described 'a gradual awareness that there was "life" in the church I attended which I knew nothing of.' Another was 'immensely attracted by the Christian love and friendship of the believers in the church fellowship to which I belonged.'

---

[47] The first stage of this study has been completed, and its fruits have been published in *Planning for Mission*, edited by Thomas Wieser.

And the more mixed the congregation is, especially in 'class' and 'colour', the greater its opportunity to demonstrate the power of Christ. A truly inter-racial, inter-social Christian fellowship, whose members evidently care for one another and bear one another's burdens, is in itself an eloquent witness to the reconciling power of Jesus Christ. This is one of the themes of the Epistle to the Ephesians. Only 'the immeasurable greatness of God's power',[48] exhibited in the resurrection of Christ, could break down 'the dividing wall of hostility' and unite Jew and Gentile 'in one body'.[49] It was miraculous. So is the overcoming of the barriers of race and rank today.

This is no doubt what Jesus meant when He said, 'By this all men will know that you are my disciples, if you have love for one another,' and when He prayed 'that they may all be one; even as thou, Father, art in me, and I in thee, that they also may be in us, so that the world may believe that thou hast sent me.'[50] It is by their divine love that Christ's disciples are known, and by their divine life that Christ Himself is believed. Speaking of the first Christian communities, Abbé Michonneau wrote: 'They were not recognized by the "culture" in which they lived, but by the love with which they loved one another, in the love of the same God.'[51]

The same truth is expressed even more forcibly if we bring together verses from John's Gospel (1:18) and John's First Epistle (4:12). Both begin with identical words: 'No man has ever seen God.' This is exactly the problem of an unbelieving world, whose philosophy is that 'seeing is

[48] Eph. 1:19.
[49] Eph. 2:14-16.
[50] John 13:35; 17:21.
[51] *Revolution in a City Parish*, p. 18.

believing'. How can they believe in an invisible God? God's first answer was to make Himself visible in His Son: 'No one has ever seen God; the only Son . . . he has made him known.'[52] As a result of the incarnation, Jesus could say 'he who has seen me has seen the Father.'[53] But still the unbeliever is not satisfied. Even if Jesus did appear as 'the image of the invisible God',[54] He has now disappeared again, so that God has once more become invisible. How then can God be seen today? John's answer is staggering: 'No man has ever seen God; if we love one another, God abides in us and his love is perfected in us.'[55] In other words, the unseen God who revealed Himself in His Son now reveals Himself in His people, in their love for one another which is nothing but the love of God. Or, as Jesus put it: 'I glorified thee on earth . . . I am glorified in them.'[56] That is, the Christ who once manifested the Father is Himself now manifested in the Church.

This is theory. How does it work out in practice? Certainly first and foremost in Christian homes and families, each of which is a microcosm of the local church. In 1958 the Lambeth bishops described the Christian home as 'a place where the sinner and the helpless may make their distress known and may be led to take the first step on the road to recovery and restoration to fellowship'.[57]

Then the influence of the Christian home is extended if it becomes the regular meeting place of a number of church members, a 'home group' or 'fellowship group' or 'house

[52] John 1:18.
[53] John 14:9.
[54] Col. 1:15.
[55] I John 4:12.
[56] John 17:4, 10.
[57] p. 2.113.

church'. If a large congregation is broken up into such groups, and if they meet weekly, fortnightly or monthly in people's homes, not only are the believers built up but unbelievers from the locality can be introduced to it and can see for themselves, perhaps for the first time, the reality, depth and integrating power of divine love.

The love which is of God and reveals God is not restricted to 'fellowship', however; it expresses itself in service also. *Philadelphia* (love of the brethren) is a particular form of *agape* (love), but not its only form. Too much Christian service is self-service, a kind of mutual benevolent scheme. But the Church is called to serve the community, not just itself. It is beautifully honouring to Christ when His followers follow His example, put on the slave's apron and perform acts of lowly service in His name. The love that serves must be spontaneous, genuine, and without affectation,[58] and not artificially contrived in order to impress or gain a hearing for the gospel.

Secondly, the local church bears witness by its worship. Naturally worship is an end in itself, as the congregation are lifted into the heavens and praise the name of the Lord. Nevertheless, indirectly a Christian congregation at worship makes a strong evangelistic impact on unbelievers. The reason for this is not far to seek. The local church is 'God's temple' in which God's Spirit dwells.[59] He does not live in temples made with hands; the only dwelling place to which He has bound and pledged Himself is His people. 'We are the temple of the living God; as God said, "I will live in them and move among them, and I will be their God, and they shall be my people".'[60] So where they

[58] Cf. Rom. 12:9.
[59] I Cor. 3:16.
[60] II Cor. 6:16.

are, He is. When the church building is empty, it is not the house of God, for He is not there (except in the sense that He is everywhere). But when the people assemble for worship, He is there. He lives in the Church, not the church.

And when Christian people meet for worship, with their Lord in their midst, and bow down before Him in humble reverence and sincerity, non-Christian people present cannot remain untouched. One young man says he was first attracted to Christ by 'hearing somebody pray extempore with arresting conviction', while the interest of an advertising manager of twenty-five was first aroused by 'attending a service where God seemed to be very real to people'.

It is not in the least necessary for the congregation to be large in order to experience the reality of God's presence. On the contrary it is when only 'two or three' gather together in Christ's name that He has specially promised to be among them.[61] Perhaps Christian congregations need to be reminded more often of these great truths today, so that we may come together expectantly, knowing that His presence will be granted, and praying that it may be manifested. Too seldom is a church able to echo Jacob's words at Bethel: 'Surely the LORD is in this place . . . How awesome is this place! This is none other than the house of God, and this is the gate of heaven.'[62]

Something should also be said in this context about preaching. When the Word preached is God's Word, the sermon becomes a means of grace to those who listen with believing hearts. Through it the living God Himself con-

[61] Matt. 18:20.
[62] Gen. 28:16 f.

74

fronts the congregation and speaks to them. The preacher can describe what is happening either as 'we beseech you on behalf of Christ' or as 'God making his appeal through us'.[63] Both are true. And it is when God's Word is thus heard that an unbeliever who enters is brought to conviction: 'the secrets of his heart are disclosed; and so, falling on his face, he will worship God and declare that God is really among you'.[64]

CONGREGATIONAL EVANGELISM

Thirdly, the local church bears witness by its direct evangelistic initiatives in the neighbourhood.

To begin with, the congregation ought to be identified as far as possible with the community, although the experience of most churches in this area seems to have been largely a failure. Few have even attempted what has been done so gallantly by the East Harlem Protestant Parish in New York. The pains, pleasures and perils of this experiment are movingly described by Bruce Kenrick in *Come Out the Wilderness*.[65] They themselves prefer the word 'participation' to describe the ideal they set themselves, reserving 'identification' for the activity of God. Certainly their fundamental philosophy, in the words of East Harlem residents, was that 'if God wasn't interested in their world (plumbing and all), then they just weren't interested in God—he was irrelevant'.[66]

Next comes the realization that parochial evangelism is not to be equated with the organization of a spasmodic mission, but is meant by God to be a continuing activity

[63] II Cor. 5:20.
[64] I Cor. 14:24 f.
[65] Collins, 1962; Fontana, 1965.
[66] *Op. cit.*, p. 29.

of the local church. It is inconceivable that a church should come together to worship only once in five years; why then should witness be thought of as a quinquennial enterprise? Worship and witness are twins, and both are unceasing functions of the Church. Tom Allan stated this excellently: 'True and effective mission is not an occasional or sporadic effort, but a continuous and coherent pattern of life within the Church. I might have called this chapter "Planning a Missionary Parish" rather than "Planning a Parish Mission", because it is my profound conviction that part at least of the ineffectiveness of our evangelism is due to our regarding it as a "special" activity to be undertaken at certain times, and not as the constant and spontaneous and inevitable outflow of our Christian experience. It is with the emergence of the missionary parish that the future of evangelism lies.'[67]

In these words Tom Allan was echoing what Abbé Michonneau had discovered in a Parisian suburb a few years earlier and had written in *Revolution in a City Parish*. According to Canon E. W. Southcott, Abbé Michonneau 'disapproved of the English title given to his book, and he would have preferred *The Parish—A Revolutionary Community*'.[68] Certainly he wrote words very similar to Tom Allan's: 'A parish in a mission country must be a missionary parish.'[69]

If local church evangelism is to be continuous, it must be congregational. Everybody should be involved in it; nobody should be allowed to stand aside. It means mobilizing the laity—all of them, or at least as many as are prepared to take part. And my experience is that they

[67] *The Face of My Parish*, p. 86.
[68] *The Parish Comes Alive*, p. 17.
[69] p. 8.

are prepared, even anxious, to take part. It is not that the overworked clergy beg the laity to help them in their work; it is rather that clergy and laity together seek to discover and then to do the will of God for the people of God as revealed in the Word of God.

A church engaged in continuing, congregational evangelism is likely to have at least three marks—a training programme, house-to-house visitation, and regular evangelistic 'guest services'.

First, training. The second proposal in the 'Recommendations and Findings' appendix of *Towards the Conversion of England* is that the clergy must 'fulfil their primary responsibility of training the laity for evangelism'.[70] William Temple's statement had been even stronger: 'the main duty of the clergy must be to train the lay members of the congregation in their work of witness.'[71]

This emphasis is certainly biblical. The whole traditional concept of 'laity' and 'ministry' has been askew, as if 'laity' were a lesser and lower breed, and as if 'ministry' belonged to clergy alone. But this distinction cannot be maintained from Scripture. The scriptural teaching is that ministry belongs to the laity and that the laity are the whole people (*laos*) of God. Indeed the function of those called to the pastorate is precisely to help the laity to fulfil their ministry. This truth emerges clearly from Ephesians 4:12, provided that the verse is punctuated correctly. The Authorized Version and Revised Standard Version both supply two commas and a stop, implying that Christ's bestowal of spiritual gifts (appointing, for example,

[70] p. 150.
[71] p. 36.

77

'pastors' and 'teachers') had a threefold purpose, namely 'the equipment of the saints', 'the work of ministry', and 'building up the body of Christ'. But Armitage Robinson has argued in his commentary on Ephesians that the first comma should be erased: 'the second of these clauses must be taken as dependent on the first, and not . . . as co-ordinate with it.'[72] This leaves us with two purposes of the pastorate, immediate and ultimate. Quoting the New English Bible, the immediate purpose is 'to equip God's people for work in his service', and the ultimate 'to the building up of the body of Christ'. Indeed, 'if the life and growth of the Body is to be secured, every member of it, and not only those who are technically called "ministers", must be taught to serve'.[73]

So 'the work of ministry' is not a clerical prerogative. It belongs inalienably to the laity, and it is the clergy's task to equip them for it. Naturally the clergy too are called to service, but 'their service is specially designed to promote the service in due measure of the rest'.[74]

How? It is my conviction that every church, either singly or in local groups, should aim to mount an annual training course or lay leadership class, until it becomes as accepted a part of the church's regular programme as the baptism and confirmation class.

Perhaps I may speak from personal experience here. Since 1950 we have held an annual training school. It consists of twelve lectures, one a week, on the theology of the gospel and the practice of evangelism. This is the syllabus:

---

[72] J. Armitage Robinson: *St. Paul's Epistle to the Ephesians* (Macmillan, 1903), p. 99. Cf. also his commentary on this verse, on p. 182.

[73] *Op. cit.*, p. 99.

[74] *Op. cit.*, p. 99.

The Theology of the Gospel

1. God
2. Man
3. Jesus Christ
4. The Cross
5. The Holy Spirit
6. The Church

The Practice of Evangelism

7. How to be fit for the Master's use
8. How to persevere when discouraged
9. How to lead a friend to Christ
10. How to meet common objections
11. How to speak for Christ
12. How to visit in homes

We begin each year in October, after the conclusion of the summer holidays, and finish (with a break over Christmas) in February. We seek to draw people's attention to it both publicly by announcement and privately by personal invitation. We keep a note throughout the year of people who ought to be encouraged to enrol. This will include such people as those who have professed conversion and made good progress since, and the members of the previous year's confirmation class.

A duplicated summary of each lecture is given to the trainees, and loose-leaf books are on sale, into which these and their own notes can be inserted. At the end of the training school comes the written examination. We make no apology for it. It helps people to take their training seriously, enables us to keep the standard high, and provides a valuable safeguard against the recruitment for responsible service in the Church of people who are either manifestly unconverted or equally manifestly odd.

The exam is taken by the candidates in their own homes.

We do not invigilate them. We tell them that they can use their Bibles as much as they like, but we trust them not to refer to the lecture summaries or their own notes, and not to seek any other help.

Those who pass the exam are 'commissioned' by our bishop, who kindly comes each year for the simple commissioning.[75] They are then issued with a commissioning certificate.[76] And each 'commissioned worker' is allotted (after consultation) some specific task in the spiritual work of the church. This is his 'commissioned service'. If he has not been commissioned, he is not eligible to do it; if he gives it up, he must resign his commission.

The scheme is not exempt from dangers. There is the danger of over-organizing, and so of stifling free initiatives. There is the danger of encouraging rivalries and jealousies. Certainly care and flexibility are needed in administering the scheme. But it has the considerable advantage of closing the back door into the privileged work of the church. One of the disgraceful features of modern church life is that in many places Sunday school teachers, club leaders, visitors and others are allowed, even encouraged, to begin their work without any (even elementary) training. A scheme of training, examining, and commissioning ensures that every authorized church worker has received at least a minimum of preparation.

Commissioned service includes house-to-house visiting, old people's welfare visiting, sick visiting, Sunday school and Bible class teaching, youth club leadership, counselling, and the leadership of fellowship groups and instruction classes. We found it necessary quite early on to make a

[75] See Appendix 1 for the form of commissioning which we use.
[76] See Appendix 2.

decision of principle as to which tasks should be included in commissioned service and which excluded. For example, some pressure was put upon us to make choir members commissioned workers, and at the same time not to require old people's welfare visitors to attend the training school and be commissioned. But after careful consideration we felt bound to disagree with both these requests. Our rough and ready principle is that every commissioned worker is expected in the course of his service to open his mouth in testimony to Jesus Christ. This therefore includes old people's visitors, who seek the eternal spiritual welfare of the 'shut-in' people they visit, as well as their temporal social welfare, whereas choir members, although they open their mouths all right, do so for worship rather than for witness!

LAY VISITING

The second feature of a local church engaged in continuous, congregational evangelism will be a systematic programme of lay visitation. In countries like England and Scotland, in which there is a national church, the whole territory is divided up into parishes. This arrangement has the unique advantage of making every single inhabitant the spiritual responsibility of some parish minister. But his 'cure of souls', especially in a large urban parish of twenty, thirty or even forty thousand people, cannot possibly be discharged by himself alone, even if he has a salaried staff. Nor is it right that he should monopolize the task and attempt the impossible. Although he will want to do some visiting of unchurched people himself, it is a good principle for the congregation to be entrusted to the minister, and the parish to the congregation. The minister is chiefly the pastor of a flock; it is pastor and flock together who should seek for Christ's sheep who are scattered abroad.

Such a method is not only right and expedient, but effective also. 'If there were a congregation,' writes Abbé Michonneau, 'which would devote itself exclusively to a door-to-door preaching of Christ, without any secondary motive, we believe that a tremendous uprising of Christianity would result.'[77] In theory I also believe that this is so, although I cannot pretend that our experience in London has been rewarded with such a dramatic result. Nevertheless I do know of a number of people reached for Christ by lay visiting. I think of an old age pensioner who for forty-three years had been a machine-minder in a Fleet Street printing works, and who through the faithfulness of his visitors opened the door of his heart to Christ; he is now a regular worshipper, and he keeps in his humble flat a picture of Holman Hunt's *The Light of the World*, to remind him of his conversion. Then there is the young Indian from South Africa who came to London with his wife and baby, was 'discovered' by house-to-house visitors, and within months was rejoicing in Christ, having been both baptized and confirmed.

There is nothing special or original about our organization. We have simply divided the parish into three areas, and appointed to each a team of visitors (all commissioned workers) under the direction of a lay District Superintendent. The visitors go out two by two, in apostolic style, calling on each house or flat in the street or block allocated to them. They seek not only to make contact with residents and gain entry into homes, nor only to cull information

[77] *Revolution in a City Parish*, p. 103.

about children, young people, the sick and the aged, nor only to invite people to church, but definitely to bear witness to Christ. They may also leave some literature. They will certainly continue to pray for those visited and in due course revisit promising spiritual contacts.

Such door-to-door visiting is hard and difficult. It is tiring after a day's work. At times the reception is chilly, at others there is no reception at all but rather a rebuff. The visitors have to be sustained by much faith, love and perseverance. We have found, therefore, that routine visiting needs to be supplemented by occasional special enterprises.

Once or twice a year we have arranged a 'visiting campaign', one night a week for three or four weeks, in which the whole visiting team and the staff have co-operated. We have supper together first and then, after briefing and prayer, go out visiting in pairs, returning to give reports and share experiences. The campaign ends with an evangelistic meeting, either a Sunday service or an informal midweek 'at home', to which all those visited are invited. Another method, on which we have just launched as I write, is a 'parish survey'. Employing the technique of social survey teams, the visitors are taking a special questionnaire into each home.[78] Its purpose is not only (or even mainly) to supply us with information, but especially to open up spiritual conversations and to make possible the distribution of a gospel booklet to nearly every home in the parish. Already visitors are finding that families, which for several years have not allowed them over the doorstep, have now invited them into the home, turned off the television and stopped the dog barking, in

[78] See Appendix 3.

83

order to give honest and thoughtful answers to the direct questions of the survey.

In some areas, in which churches of different denominations are situated, inter-church visiting teams are possible. We have also conducted visiting campaigns in other, less privileged parishes. And some years ago we seconded teams of commissioned workers to two other churches, to act as a kind of 'spiritual blood transfusion'. This experiment was considered at least a partial success. It was certainly costly to those who took part in it. It also led to the permanent transfer of at least one team member to the church visited and to his licensing as a parochial reader in that church. Indeed one of the side-effects of all this visiting, as of other forms of commissioned service, is to foster vocation to the ministry and the mission field. A number of our former commissioned workers are in such 'full-time' service today. It seems true to say that God seldom calls people to a wider ministry before they have first proved themselves in a narrower; and the best and most natural context in which to put to the test an incipient sense of vocation is the regular evangelistic outreach of the local church.

GUEST SERVICES

This brings me to the third feature of a church engaged in continuing, congregational evangelism, namely 'guest services'. Such is the convenient name, widely adopted in England, for services to which church members are urged to bring a guest. It is, of course, the tradition of many churches, especially Free Churches, to regard the evening service as always evangelistic in purpose. Many assemblies of Christian Brethren, for example, 'break bread' together every Sunday morning and hold a gospel service every Sunday evening. This practice has much to commend it, and one cannot but admire the evangelistic zeal which it expresses. On the other hand it has disadvantages. One is that there are believers who for various reasons cannot worship on Sunday mornings and who therefore need the ministry of the Word themselves on Sunday evenings. Another is that 'familiarity breeds contempt'. If the minister prepares and delivers an evangelistic sermon every Sunday night, without doubt he will sometimes find himself preaching conversion only to the converted.

One value of more occasional evangelistic services, whether held at regular intervals or just once or twice a year, is that special preparations can be made for them. Prayer will be concentrated on them. And, since they are advertised well in advance, the congregation knows when they are to be held and can take pains to invite and bring with them to church a relative, friend, colleague or neighbour.

It is perfectly true that, because of the general decline in churchgoing in many parts of the world, 'pulpit preaching can no longer be relied on as the principal medium for evangelization', since 'you cannot convert people who are not there'.[79] For this reason we should probably be doing more open-air preaching, where the unconverted people are, as well as seeking to visit them at home and witness to them at work. Nevertheless many non-churchgoers will still for friendship's sake accept an invitation to a special guest service. It is certainly a heart-warming privilege to present the good news to a congregation which is known to contain a substantial proportion of unbelievers.

[79] *Towards the Conversion of England*, p. 3.

A guest service may take many forms, but at least it will be simple, and as relevant as possible to the condition of the unconverted. When the time comes for the sermon, the preacher will ignore any Christians who may happen to be present. He will assume no previous knowledge on the part of the congregation, and will seek from the Scriptures to 'proclaim', 'explain', 'argue' and 'prove'[80] some fundamental parts of the gospel. He will go further, if his preaching is biblical, and 'beg' his listeners on behalf of Christ to be reconciled to God.[81]

Opinions differ as to what opportunity, if any, should be given to people to respond publicly to the message. We must at all costs avoid the faithless and fleshly attempt to usurp the Holy Spirit's prerogatives and do His work for Him. Speaking personally, I believe that a legitimate distinction may be drawn between pressing people to take some step for which the Holy Spirit has not made them ready (which is as harmful as it is wrong) and, on the other hand, giving them an opportunity to make public the fact of their response to Christ, which is what the Holy Spirit is calling them to do.

The preacher may clinch the issue of response in different ways. He may invite people to write to him, or come and see him in his home or vestry. Or he may leave a sheet of paper at the back of the church on which they may enter their name and address if they would like further help or a visit. Or he may suggest that they ask him for a booklet as they leave church.

But in our case, now for over fifteen years, we have concluded every monthly guest service with a so-called

---

[80] Cf. Acts 17:2 f. (R.S.V.) for these verbs.
[81] II Cor. 5:20; 6:1.

'continuation service'. This is a cumbersome title for a brief, voluntary, quarter-of-an-hour epilogue. Its purpose is candidly stated during the notices, 'to give the preacher the opportunity to explain simply and directly what it means to be a committed Christian and how to receive Christ'. The invitation to stay behind is repeated at the end of the sermon. Our experience is that, when the rest of the congregation leaves, many do stay—some of their own accord, others because the Christian friend who has brought them suggests it.

The preacher then has the golden opportunity of expounding the way of salvation to a group of interested enquirers and of outlining the steps to Christ. This is the time, if he is faithful to the biblical gospel, to speak of sin, guilt and judgment, of God's love and Christ's cross, of repentance and faith, and of the cost of Christian discipleship.

The continuation service may be ended in a variety of ways. There is no one stereotyped method to be recommended. We ourselves do not always follow the same pattern. And the very thought of rigid patterns is distasteful. Nevertheless our normal custom is to invite the congregation to kneel to pray, sometimes in complete silence, sometimes echoing silently the preacher's prayer. This moment of response is most sacred, and great spiritual sensitivity is needed, lest we intrude clumsily into the Spirit's preserve or into the enquirer's privacy.

Those who have come to Christ in the secrecy of their own hearts, or have sincerely echoed the preacher's prayer, are then invited to come forward. No pressure of any kind is exerted, but reasons for the suggestion are given. The preacher says he would like to meet those who have trusted

Christ, to give them a booklet and to introduce them to a counsellor. Besides this, he adds, they would find this simple step the chance to confess Christ openly and to burn their boats.

The counsellors are all commissioned workers, who have also received some further training. They not only give elementary spiritual advice to the enquirer about faith, prayer, Bible reading and church attendance, but also obtain some basic information about his name, occupation, address, and so on.

Those who profess faith in Christ at a guest service are invited to an 'at home' about a week later, at which a talk is given on Christian life and growth. They are also told about our so-called 'nursery classes'. This strange and rather daunting expression describes special classes for new Christians. Being new-born babes in Christ, their place is after all in the spiritual nursery! Nursery class leaders are mostly lay people (commissioned workers again), to whom is entrusted the privileged task of nurturing the lambs of Christ's flock. In these classes the new Christians learn how to read the Bible and pray, and are gradually drawn into the fellowship of the congregation.

I have ventured in this chapter to go into some considerable practical detail, in order to illustrate how the local church is the divine agency in mission. It is not only through the personal witness, at home and at work, of its individual members. It is also through the corporate witness of the congregation, through the brotherly love of its fellowship, the godly sincerity of its worship, and the continuous collective outreach of its evangelism.

CHAPTER FOUR

THE SPIRIT OF GOD

THE EVANGELISTIC DYNAMIC

Evangelism is hard work. With this everybody who has attempted to engage in it will agree. Whether the agent is the evangelistic preacher or the individual witness, he often finds like Ezekiel that his hearers are 'rebels . . ., impudent and stubborn', men 'of a hard forehead and of a stubborn heart'.[1] Sometimes they are actively hostile. More frequently they are icily indifferent. Their minds are entrenched in prejudice and their affections intoxicated with pleasure. Their defences appear to be completely impenetrable. The evangelist scatters his precious seed, but some of it bounces off the surface of men's hearts. Or it gains such a minimal entry that it is immediately scorched by the fires of tribulation or suffocated by the rival attractions of the world. Truly, souls are hardly won.

Disappointment and discouragement are perilous companions to live with. Under their influence some men resort to illicit means in a determined effort to make their evangelism effective. They invent various stunts to attract people to services or meetings. They develop and perfect evangelistic techniques, conveying the impression that souls can be satisfactorily processed like the products of the local factory. Or they exert personality-pressure on their victims, trying by bombast, by rhetoric, by emotion

[1] Ezek. 2:3, 4; 3:7.

without reason, to bully them into submission to Christ. In a word, they rely on the energy of the flesh instead of the power of the Spirit. To do this is to expose oneself to the strictures of Dr. William Sargant who argues in his celebrated *Battle for the Mind*[2] that there is nothing much to choose between some forms of Christian evangelism and the horrors of Communist brainwashing.

Zeal for the glory of God, loyalty to the biblical gospel, and the mobilization of the local church will not in themselves promote successful evangelism or win men for Christ. Only the Holy Spirit can do that. For 'the Spirit is the witness, because the Spirit is the truth'.[3] And without the power of His divine witness all human witness is impotent. 'The Spirit is the great interpreter who can break all sound and language barriers'[4] and communicate the gospel with effect.

One of the classical definitions of evangelism, that formulated by the *Archbishops' Committee of Enquiry on the Evangelistic Work of the Church* (1918) and adopted in *Towards the Conversion of England* (1945),[5] affirms that 'to evangelize is so to present Christ Jesus in the power of the Holy Spirit, that men shall come to put their trust in God through Him . . .' Dr. J. I. Packer has rightly criticized the introduction of 'a consecutive clause where a final clause should be'. To say that evangelism is 'so to present Christ Jesus in the power of the Holy Spirit, that men shall come . . .' instead of 'to present Christ Jesus . . . in order that, through the power of the Holy Spirit,

[2] Published by Heinemann in 1957. But compare the criticism of much of Dr. Sargant's thesis in Dr. D. M. Lloyd-Jones' *Conversions Psychological and Spiritual* (I.V.F., 1959).
[3] I John 5:7.
[4] *What is Evangelism?*, pp. 81 f.
[5] p. 1.

men may come . . .', he goes on, is 'to define evangelism in terms of an effect achieved in the lives of others, which amounts to saying that the essence of evangelizing is producing converts', whereas in fact 'evangelism is just preaching the gospel, the evangel'.[6] This is a just criticism. Nevertheless, we are thankful for the prominent place given to the Holy Spirit in the definition.

EVANGELISM AND REVIVAL

Having asserted that the winning of converts to Jesus Christ is the work of the Holy Spirit, we must now distinguish between His extraordinary and His ordinary operations, that is to say, between 'revival' and 'evangelism'. Both are supernatural, since the quickening of a dead soul is a miracle of grace, not a process of nature; but revival is a special movement of the Holy Spirit. In a season of revival God so 'visits' a district that the whole community becomes aware of His presence and absorbed in spiritual realities previously neglected. Conviction of sin, repentance, conversion, the joy of salvation, brotherly love and growth in holiness all become commonplace. Formidable barriers to the spread of the gospel are removed. Hardened sinners are softened, the irredeemable redeemed and the irreformable reformed. In the figurative language of Scripture, when God's people Israel became 'his sanctuary' and 'his dominion'—the place where He was both dwelling and reigning—then 'the sea looked and fled, Jordan turned back, the mountains skipped like rams, the hills like lambs'. Why? Answer: 'Tremble, O earth, at the presence of the LORD, at the presence of the God of Jacob . . .'[7]

---

[6] *Evangelism and the Sovereignty of God*, pp. 40 f.
[7] Ps. 114.

Such 'revival' is a sovereign work of God. True, history teaches the lesson that a time of revival is normally preceded by a time of spiritual deadness and drought in which God's people begin with increasing fervour to humble themselves before Him, to hunger and thirst for Him, and to long for His intervention. Nevertheless, revival is neither at the command nor under the control of men.

Must evangelism wait for revival, then? No. Much as we may yearn and pray for God to 'rend the heavens and come down',[8] to vindicate the holiness of His great name by some altogether unusual visitation, the Church has no liberty meanwhile to suspend its regular evangelistic task. And this incessant evangelism is as much dependent on the power of the Spirit as is revival.

Indeed each stage of the unfolding of the gospel will be void of effect without the Holy Spirit. We saw in Chapter Two that the gospel is concerned with sin, grace and faith, that is, with man's moral need, with God's action in Christ to meet it, and with the obedience of faith by which Christ is appropriated. We must now see how the work of the Holy Spirit is essential at each stage, bringing people first to a conviction of sin, secondly to a vision of Christ, and thirdly to conversion and regeneration. We shall consider each in turn.

CONVICTION OF SIN

The first necessity, then, is a conviction of sin. It was argued in Chapter Two that, although we must be alert to discover a person's felt need, and although in fact many are converted without any great sense of sin, yet this does not relieve us of the responsibility to speak of 'righteous-

[8] Isa. 64:1.

ness, self-control and the coming judgment'.[9] Since the gospel is good news of salvation, and since salvation is deliverance from sin, we cannot bypass the subject of sin in our evangelistic witness. If we do, we are bound to distort the biblical gospel and so pervert the biblical concept of evangelism.

But how are twentieth-century people to be cured of their complacent apathy, so that they acknowledge their sin and call upon Christ to save them? Only the Holy Spirit can do it. 'When he comes,' Jesus said, 'he will convince the world of sin and of righteousness and of judgment: of sin, because they do not believe in me; of righteousness, because I go to the Father, and you will see me no more; of judgment, because the ruler of this world is judged.'[10] Sin, righteousness and judgment are the three categories of whose truth the Holy Spirit will convince people, and He will show the relation of each to Christ. Men will come to see the gravity of sin (because sinners reject Christ), the possibility of righteousness (because Christ has been accepted by the Father), and the certainty of judgment (because in Christ the devil has already been judged). Of these three moral realities, the first (sin) is primary, while the other two are the possible outcomes of it, 'righteousness' being God's justification of the penitent, and 'judgment' His condemnation of the impenitent. So only when men are brought to acknowledge their sin is it possible for them through faith in Christ to receive righteousness and escape judgment.

The means which the Holy Spirit employs to convince people of sin is the law, for 'sin is lawlessness',[11] the

[9] Acts 24:25 (Jerusalem Bible).
[10] John 16:8-11.
[11] 1 John 3:4.

infringement of the law of God. 'Through the law comes knowledge of sin'.[12] 'If it had not been for the law, I should not have known sin'.[13] It is chiefly in this sense that 'the law was our custodian until Christ came'.[14] It is only when the law condemns us that we look to Christ to justify us.

There are many nowadays who repudiate this category of law in relation both to sin and to the atonement. It introduces forensic concepts, they say, which are meaningless to the majority. With this we emphatically disagree. Biblical references to 'law' do not date, because they do not relate to Jewish, Roman, feudal or British law but to the timeless law of God, which is simply the expression of His unchanging nature. Moreover, men readily understand what 'law' is because it is a universal phenomenon. Wherever human society exists, law operates and citizens are familiar with its authority, its enforcement, and its penalties.

THE PLACE OF THE LAW

Before we preach the gospel, then, we must preach the law. Indeed this has never been more necessary than it is today when we are witnessing a widespread revolt against authority. The gospel can only justify those whom the law condemns. These are the respective functions of law and gospel; as Luther put it, it is the work of the law to 'terrify', and the work of the gospel to 'justify'.[15] Thus every man's spiritual history becomes a microcosm of God's dealings with the human race. God did not im-

[12] Rom. 3:20.
[13] Rom. 7:7.
[14] Gal. 3:24.
[15] *Commentary on the Epistle to the Galatians* (Clarke, 1953), p. 423.

mediately send His Son; nor can we immediately preach Him. A long programme of education and preparation came first, in particular the giving of the law to expose the fact and gravity of sin. And the law still performs the same function. 'It is only when one submits to the law,' wrote Dietrich Bonhoeffer in prison 'that one can speak of grace ... I don't think it is Christian to want to get to the New Testament too soon or too directly.'[16] To bypass the law is to cheapen the gospel. We must meet Moses before we are ready to meet Christ.

In practice therefore we should not be afraid to expound the law. On the contrary we must constantly hold up before the eyes of men the unchanging standards of God, His inflexible demands, and their summary in the paramount commandments to love God with all our being and our neighbour as ourselves.

But if the Holy Spirit uses the law to convince sinners of their sin, how are we to bring a knowledge of the law to those who are outside the Church? Are we to engrave or paint the ten commandments on the external walls of the church building, or print them on posters, or recite them to passers-by, or declaim them from an open-air soap-box? We should certainly not despise any of these methods. Yet God has also chosen other means to acquaint people with His law, to convert an abstract notion into a concrete reality.

The first is Christ Himself. Jesus was 'born under the law',[17] and from His circumcision on the eighth day of His life to His death on the cross He perfectly obeyed the law, setting Himself 'to fulfil all righteousness'.[18] Many

[16] *Letters and Papers from Prison* (1959), p. 50.
[17] Gal. 4:4.
[18] Matt. 3:15.

people, who remain unmoved by a recitation of the ten commandments in their nakedness, are brought to a sense of sin when they see them clothed in the holy life of Jesus. Confronted by Him in the perfection of His self-mastery and self-sacrifice, we cannot help falling down at Jesus' knees with Simon Peter and crying out, 'Depart from me, for I am a sinful man, O Lord.'[19]

For example, a Jewish businessman from Hungary describes his conversion at the age of fifty-five in these words: 'When my blind eyes were opened and I beheld the love and purity of Jesus' face, my blemishes were mirrored back to me, and I saw myself, wicked sinner that I am. I saw the cross, and understood the meaning of Calvary for the first time, and I fell down in true repentance and asked the Lord Jesus to cover me with His precious blood that was shed for me as an atonement for my sins.'

If the first embodiment of the law is Christ, the second is (or should be) Christians. God's people love God's law and seek to keep it.[20] This is not the place to argue with the advocates of the so-called 'new morality', who assert that the category of law has been abolished in the Christian life. It is sufficient to say that the biblical writers would not recognize them. Far from teaching the abolition of law, the New Testament declares that God sent His Son to die for us 'in order that the just requirement of the law might be fulfilled in us',[21] and that He sends His Spirit into our hearts to write His law there.[22]

[19] Luke 5:8.
[20] Psalm 119 expresses throughout the language and sentiments of a regenerate believer.
[21] Rom. 8:4.
[22] Jer. 31:33; cf. Ezek. 36:27.

So the light of God's law, which shines at its brightest in Jesus, shines in His disciples too. And this light exposes and shames the darkness. It was so in the life of Christ: 'this is the judgment, that the light has come into the world, and men loved darkness rather than light, because their deeds were evil. For every one who does evil hates the light, and does not come to the light, lest his deeds should be exposed'.[23] The same truth is stated of Christians by the apostle Paul: 'once you were darkness, but now you are light in the Lord; walk as children of light . . . Take no part in the unfruitful works of darkness, but instead expose them.'[24] That is, the light itself shows up the works of darkness for what they are and puts them to shame.

This is not theological truth only. It happens again and again in practice. What the Holy Spirit uses to prick the unbeliever's conscience is the consistent, law-abiding, shining conduct of a Christian. A sense of shame leads to a sense of guilt, and so to Christ the sinbearer.

Let me give you an example from the life of Barclay Buxton. He was a missionary in Japan for about seventeen years and co-founder of the Japan Evangelistic Band. A year or two before he died, in his mid-eighties, he became crippled with arthritis and came up to London twice a week for physical treatment at a clinic. He thus became a familiar figure to the resident porter, who took him up and down in the lift and was deeply impressed by him. 'Who is that elderly gentleman?' he enquired of the osteopath one day. 'Why do you ask?' 'Please, sir, he makes me feel so rotten.'

[23] John 3:19, 20.
[24] Eph. 5:8-13.

97

If the Holy Spirit's first work is to convince of sin, His next is to testify to Christ. Both activities are directed towards the Christ-rejecting world. 'When he comes, he will convince the world of sin . . .', Jesus said.[25] Again 'If the world hates you, know that it has hated me before it hated you . . . But when the Counsellor comes . . . he will bear witness to me.'[26] In both passages the context of the Holy Spirit's work is the unbelieving 'world', and in both the Greek preposition is *peri*, 'concerning'. 'When he comes, he will convince the world *concerning* sin.' 'When he comes, he will bear witness *concerning* me.' The two chief topics of the Spirit's conversation with the world therefore are sin and Christ. This is what He talks about. This is what we must talk about too.

We have already had occasion to notice the order. We are accustomed to think of ourselves as the chief witnesses, who then hope and pray that the Holy Spirit will confirm our witness. Indeed this is true, as far as it goes. But here Christ reverses the order: 'he will witness concerning me; and you also will witness . . .'[27] That is, He is the principal witness, and we from our experience are to corroborate His testimony, rather than He ours.

The whole of Scripture is the Spirit's witness to the Son, especially to 'the sufferings of Christ and the subsequent glory'.[28] And as we speak of Christ from Scripture, the Holy Spirit delights to endorse His own witness. Dr. R. A. Torrey tells us in one of his books how D. L. Moody

[25] John 16:8.
[26] John 15:18, 26.
[27] John 15:26, 27 (literally).
[28] I Pet. 1:11.

described the effect of the first Christian sermon. On the day of Pentecost, when the apostle Peter bore witness to Christ out of the Scriptures, 'the Holy Spirit said "Amen" and the people saw and believed'.[29]

Canon Bryan Green's statement is incontrovertible: 'in every conversion that can rightly be called Christian some knowledge of Christ must be present'.[30] Indeed, Christ is Himself the centre of every conversion. But are we equally clear that this vision of Christ is impossible without divine revelation? When Simon Peter confessed his faith in Jesus at Caesarea Philippi, Jesus commented: 'flesh and blood has not revealed this to you, but my Father who is in heaven.'[31] These words may be applied to every conversion, without exception.

It is sometimes said that the conversion of Saul of Tarsus on the Damascus road was so abnormal as to supply no pattern for conversion today. This is true if the dramatic outward accompaniments of it are meant—the flashing light, the Hebrew-speaking voice, the falling to the ground blinded. But Saul's essential inward experience is the same for every man, as he describes it in his own words: 'it pleased God . . . to reveal his Son in me.'[32] Again, 'God . . . has shone in our hearts to give the light of the knowledge of the glory of God in the face of Christ.'[33] Every converted Christian can echo these words from his own experience. Once we were blind,[34] as blind to the glory of Christ as we were to our own sin, guilt and

[29] *The Person and Work of the Holy Spirit* by R. A. Torrey (Nisbet, 1910), p. 95.
[30] *The Practice of Evangelism*, p. 38.
[31] Matt. 16:17.
[32] Gal. 1:15, 16 (A.V.).
[33] II Cor. 4:6.
[34] II Cor. 4:3, 4; cf. John 9:25.

danger. But now our eyes have been opened to see Him as our Saviour and Lord, for 'no one can say "Jesus is Lord" except by the Holy Spirit'.[35]

CONVERSION AND REGENERATION

The third work of the Holy Spirit is the actual bringing about of that indispensable event called 'conversion' and 'regeneration'. Since much misunderstanding surrounds these words, they need to be clarified. In one sense they cannot be separated from one another. Every converted person is regenerate; every regenerate person is converted. Yet they can (and must) be distinguished. Indeed, it is impossible to answer such common questions as whether conversion is sudden or gradual until they have been carefully differentiated and clearly defined. The essential distinction, although it will need later to be qualified, is that regeneration is something which *God* does, while conversion is something which *we* do ourselves (although not by ourselves).

Regeneration is the new birth, and it is absurd to imagine that anybody could ever give birth to himself, either physically or spiritually. The new birth is a birth 'from above',[36] a birth 'of the Spirit',[37] a birth 'of God'.[38] It is God who 'begets' us,[39] putting His Spirit within us, implanting life in our souls and making us partakers of His divine nature.[40] All this is His work alone, making us in Christ a 'new creation'.[41]

[35] I Cor. 12:3.
[36] In John 3:3 and 7 *anōthen* could be translated either 'anew' (RSV) or 'from above' (RSV margin).
[37] John 3:5, 6, 8.
[38] John 1:13; I John 3:9, 4:7, etc.
[39] For example, Jas. 1:18.
[40] For example, Gal. 4:6; Eph. 2:1; II Pet. 1:4.
[41] II Cor. 5:17.

But conversion is what we do, when we 'turn' to God, as in Acts 9:35; 11:21 and 26:20. The muddle is due to the use in our English Bibles of the passive expression 'to be converted' for what in the Greek has an active sense 'to turn'. When the verb occurs in non-theological contexts it means either to 'turn' from one direction to another, as when Jesus turned round in the crowd,[42] or to 'return' from one place to another, as when the holy family returned from Jerusalem to Nazareth.[43] The theological use of the verb implies the same double movement, turning from idols to the living and true God,[44] and returning to the Shepherd and Guardian of our souls from the paths of sin to which like sheep we had strayed.[45] Since the turn from idols and sin is called *repentance*, and the turn to God and Christ *faith*, we conclude that repentance plus faith equal conversion.

Having appreciated the difference between regeneration as something God does ('begetting' or 'quickening') and conversion as something we do ('turning'), we now have to qualify the distinction by adding that, nevertheless, both are the works of God. For although we are commanded to repent and to believe,[46] and both are responsible human actions, yet we cannot do either by ourselves but only by God's grace. It is His 'kindness' which leads men to repentance,[47] and it is 'through grace' that they believe.[48] Each is a divine gift. Peter glorified God that to the Gentiles He had '*granted* repentance unto life',[49]

[42] For example, Mark 5:30.
[43] Luke 2:39.
[44] I Thess. 1:9.
[45] I Pet. 2:25.
[46] For example, Acts 17:30; 16:31.
[47] Rom. 2:4.
[48] Acts 18:27.
[49] Acts 11:18 *edōken*; cf. Acts 5:31.

and Paul told the Philippians that it had been '*granted*' them to believe in Christ.[50]

The divine givenness of repentance and faith is plain in Scripture; it is equally plain in human experience. Indeed every Christian admits it, as Dr. Packer cogently argues, by thanking God for his own conversion and by praying for the conversion of others. 'Thus,' he says to his reader, 'by your practice of intercession, no less than by giving thanks for your conversion, you acknowledge and confess the sovereignty of God's grace. And so do all Christian people everywhere . . . On our feet we may have arguments about it, but on our knees we are all agreed.'[51]

One of the most moving modern accounts of God in pursuit of man is that given by C. S. Lewis in his auto-biographical narrative *Surprised by Joy*. He mixes many metaphors in his attempt to convey his sense of it. First, God 'the great Angler played His fish, and I never dreamed that the hook was in my tongue'.[52] Next, the angler turned hunter: 'the fox had been dislodged from Hegelian Wood and was now running in the open . . . bedraggled and weary, hounds barely a field behind. And nearly everyone was now (one way and another) in the pack'.[53] So helpless does he feel that he dares even to describe God as playing with him: 'amiable agnostics will talk cheerfully about "man's search for God". To me . . . they might as well

[50] Phil. 1:29, *echaristhē*; cf. Eph. 2:8.

[51] *Evangelism and the Sovereignty of God*, pp. 12–17. The whole book is essential reading for those who wish to clarify their thinking on the relation between the doctrines of divine sovereignty and election and the practice of evangelism. Its emphasis is that 'so far from making evangelism pointless, the sovereignty of God in grace is the one thing that prevents evangelism from being pointless. For it creates the possibility—indeed, the certainty—that evangelism will be fruitful' (p. 106).

[52] *Surprised by Joy* (Bles, 1955), p. 199.

[53] p. 212.

have talked about the mouse's search for the cat'.[54] In the end the angler, the hunter and the cat give place to the invincible chess-player: 'all over the board my pieces were in the most disadvantageous positions. Soon I could no longer cherish even the illusion that the initiative lay with me. My Adversary began to make His final moves';[55] and the penultimate chapter of his book is called 'Checkmate'.

The divine victory is told in graphic terms: 'you must picture me alone in that room in Magdalen, night after night, feeling, whenever my mind lifted for a second from my work, the steady, unrelenting approach of Him whom I so earnestly desired not to meet. That which I greatly feared had at last come upon me. In the Trinity Term of 1929 I gave in, and admitted that God was God, and knelt and prayed: perhaps, that night, the most dejected and reluctant convert in all England. I did not then see what is now the most shining and obvious thing; the divine humility which will accept a convert even on such terms. The Prodigal Son at least walked home on his own feet. But who can duly adore that Love which will open the high gates to a prodigal who is brought in kicking, struggling, resentful, and darting his eyes in every direction for a chance to escape? . . . The hardness of God is kinder than the softness of men, and His compulsion is our liberation.'[56]

Our own experience may well have been less dramatic, but in its own way it is the same. We do not claim the credit for our conversion; we humbly recognize that the initiative was God's. In answer to the questionnaire already men-

[54] p. 214.
[55] p. 205.
[56] p. 215.

tioned, a middle-aged consultant physician wrote about 'the step of faith': 'I can't say I actually took one myself. Something or Somebody finally pushed me. In the middle of an argument defending my position—indeed in the middle of a sentence—I suddenly realized that I *could* accept the new life offered . . . So I just surrendered to the Cross, and *immediately* I said the words "I see".'

However, the New Testament teaching about regeneration and conversion, illustrated in authentic Christian experience, raises a number of questions. We can only consider them briefly. First, which is prior to the other? Secondly, are they sudden or gradual? Thirdly, what is their relation to baptism? Fourthly, if both are the works of God, what is the point of evangelism?

First, which is prior to the other? Some students of the New Testament, strong in their grasp of reformed theology, insist that regeneration precedes conversion, and indeed that conversion is the first fruit of regeneration. Since unbelievers are spiritually dead, it is argued, they cannot repent and believe until they have been born from above. The value of this position is its emphasis that sinners cannot turn from sin to Christ without the Holy Spirit. This is so. But the terms in which it is expressed sometimes go beyond the actual language of the New Testament. It is dangerous to argue from analogy and say 'dead men cannot . . .', because Jesus Himself said: 'the dead will hear the voice of the Son of God, and those who hear will live'.[57] Further, the order of events to which the apostles commonly bear witness is that faith is antecedent to life. It is by believing that we live.[58] Nevertheless we

[57] John 5:25.
[58] For example, John 3:15, 16; 20:31.

must add in the most emphatic terms that it is only by grace that we believe.

Secondly, are regeneration and conversion sudden or gradual? Having distinguished between them, we are only now able to answer this question. We must say that regeneration is sudden. The metaphor of birth requires this reply. Although months of gestation precede physical birth and years of development follow it, birth itself is an almost instantaneous emergence into a new life, so that everybody has a 'birthday', an actual day on which it happened. So too spiritually there is a day, even a moment, when God quickens a dead soul into life. This is not to say that it is *consciously* sudden, however. We would not know our physical birthday unless our parents had told us, and many people will never know their spiritual birthday unless their heavenly Father tells them in heaven.

But conversion may be gradual. A period of time, now long, now short, elapses between the awakening of a person's spiritual interest and concern and the time when he knows he is a repentant believer in Christ. This interim period is variously described: 'In a short time you think to make me a Christian!'[59] 'I believe; help my unbelief'.[60] 'You are not far from the kingdom of God'.[61] We have all met people in this betwixt and between stage, almost persuaded, in the twilight of faith, not far from the kingdom. However, there comes a moment, usually known only to God, when impenitence gives way to repentance and unbelief to faith, and the believer is regenerate. Not of course that this is the end, for birth

[59] Acts 26:28.
[60] Mark 9:24.
[61] Mark 12:34.

is followed by growth and justification by sanctification, but it is an indispensable beginning.

One of the questions I put to members of our church, in the questionnaire already mentioned, was 'how long a period elapsed between the awakening of your interest and your conversion?' Only five claimed a really sudden conversion, on the same day, and five more within a few days. Ten measured the period in weeks, twenty-seven in months and forty-three in years. The remaining fifteen could not remember, mostly because they had been born and bred in a Christian home.

BAPTISM

Thirdly, what is the relation between conversion and regeneration on the one hand and baptism on the other? It is not possible here to digress at length into the theology of baptism.[62] But something must be said on this subject because of its practical implications for evangelism. Some evangelists vary their message according to whether their listeners are baptized or unbaptized. This is logical however only if baptism secures our regeneration, bestows life and places us in Christ. It is plainly impossible to summon people to 'come to Christ' if they are already 'in Christ' by baptism; we can then only invite them to return to Him if they have strayed, or to grow up in Him if they are immature.

Let me cut the Gordian knot and declare that baptism and regeneration are not the same thing, that the one neither conveys nor secures the other, that there are

[62] See for an introduction, *Right to Baptize* by Geoffrey Hart (Hodder and Stoughton, 1966), No. 15 in the *Christian Foundations* series.

baptized people who are not spiritually regenerate, and also, although this is (to say the least) irregular, that there are some regenerate people who are not baptized. Let me emphasize, further, that neither Bible nor Prayer Book teaches that baptism effects regeneration. The expressions in the baptism service which have given rise to this view (for example 'seeing now . . . that this child/person is regenerate') can be properly interpreted only in the light of the whole service. To isolate a text from its context is as irresponsible in the Prayer Book as it is in the Bible. We need to ask ourselves: who is this person who is declared regenerate? It is not just somebody who has been baptized in the name of the Trinity, but somebody who, before being baptized, has publicly professed his repentance, faith and submission, either with his own mouth or (in the case of a child) through the lips of his sponsors. Whether the reformers were right to represent a child as thus speaking is another matter; the point here is that the only children baptized in the Church of England, and the only adults, are *professed believers*. And this is why they are declared regenerate. They are regenerate in the same sense in which they are penitent believers in Christ. This is the hypothetical language which is proper to the administration of sacraments, and which the New Testament itself uses when it attributes to baptism what it elsewhere attributes to grace and faith.[63]

The Book of Common Prayer and the Articles teach not a mechanical *ex opere operato* view of the sacraments, but a 'receptionist' view, namely that their effect depends upon their reception, in particular upon a believing reception: 'in such only as worthily receive the same they have a

[63] For example, Rom. 6:3, 4; Gal. 3:26, 27; I Pet. 3:21.

wholesome effect or operation'.[64] It is in this way that we must explain the baptismal language of the Prayer Book, and not by diluting the meaning of regeneration as if it signified only the planting of a seed (conception as opposed to birth), or only admission into the Christian society, for we have no authority to whittle down the biblical meaning of regeneration into anything less than a birth from God.

So baptism, which admits people into the visible church (the company of the baptized), does not admit to the invisible ('the blessed company of all faithful people', that is, of believers). It is the sacrament of regeneration, visibly signifying and pledging it, but not the means of regeneration, invariably conveying it. Therefore in evangelism we can summon baptized people to come to Christ, or at least to make sure they have come to Christ, in order to claim for themselves in reality by faith what is already theirs in baptism by title. It is refreshing to read the statements of the Abbé Michonneau (although I do not know if he accepts the full implications of what he writes) that among the French industrial proletariat 'the mentality of those who have been baptized . . . is no different from that of the non-baptized. The conduct of both is the same. We can consider both as pagans'. His conclusion is therefore: 'we have to deal with a parish which is a mission parish in a mission land.'[65]

The fourth question which we must ask about conversion and regeneration is this: if both are the works of God, what is the point of evangelism?

We must not answer this by weakening the biblical

[64] Article XXV *Of the Sacraments.*
[65] *Revolution in a City Parish*, pp. 1-3.

doctrine of human inability. It is grievously mistaken to suggest that the purpose of evangelism is to cajole sinners into doing what they can perfectly well do if only they put their minds to it and pull themselves together. This the Bible emphatically denies. Consider these two statements: 'No one can say "Jesus is Lord" except by the Holy Spirit'.[66] 'No one can come to me unless the Father . . . draws him'.[67] We need to hear much more in the Church of this 'no one can', this natural inability of men to believe in Christ or to come to Christ. Only the Spirit can reveal Christ to men; only the Father can draw men to Christ. And without this double work of the Father and the Spirit no one can reach the Son. It is quite true that Jesus also said 'you are not willing to come to me that you may have life',[68] and that the human mind finds it impossible neatly to resolve the tension between this 'cannot' and this 'will not'. But both are true, and man's refusal to come does not cancel out his inability without grace to do so.

The practical importance of recovering the doctrine of human inability is that without it the evangelist becomes self-confident. Much of our evangelism is vitiated by this spirit, caused by bad theology. The New Testament portrait of man without Christ is that his heart is hard (he does not feel his sin), his eyes are blind (he does not see Christ), and his will is enslaved (he cannot turn to God). Moreover if the sinner cannot do these things, neither can the evangelist do them for him. Therefore the work of the Spirit is indispensable. It is not given to men to open the eyes of the blind or to give life to the dead.

[66] I Cor. 12:3; cf. I Cor. 2:14.
[67] John 6:44; cf. Rom. 8:7.
[68] John 5:40 (literally); cf. Matt. 23:37.

Only the Holy Spirit can do this. We must repeat that conversion and regeneration are His works.

THE POINT OF EVANGELISM

This brings us back to our fourth question: then what is the point of evangelism? I do not know a better way of answering this question than by referring the reader to II Corinthians 4:4-6. In this passage the apostle Paul describes in graphic terms both the condition of the unconverted and the marvel of conversion. Here are the unconverted: 'the god of this world (Satan, who of course is a usurper and no god at all) has blinded the minds of unbelievers'. Indeed, their state is likened to the primeval chaos of Genesis 1:2 before the Creator began to reduce it to order. Everything was formless, empty and dark, until God's creative fiat rang out in the night: 'Let there be light,' and there was light. Conversion is like that, says Paul. 'It is the God who said, "Let light shine out of darkness," who has shone in our hearts to give the light of the knowledge of the glory of God in the face of Christ.'

Here then are two 'gods' in opposition, 'the god of this world' and the God and Father of our Lord Jesus Christ. The god of this world, being the prince of darkness, has blinded the minds of unbelievers, whereas the God and Father of our Lord Jesus Christ, being the God of light, shines into men's hearts. This is the unseen spiritual warfare, the conflict over the souls of men. In view of it, one might argue, would it not be both modest and prudent for us to withdraw from the field of battle and leave these two 'gods' to fight it out? What can we frail humans hope to contribute? But the apostle reaches a very different conclusion. Between verses 4 and 6, which we have so far considered, he writes: 'we preach . . . Jesus Christ.' The sovereign grace of God, far from making preaching unnecessary, actually makes it indispensable. The 'light' which the devil keeps men from seeing and which God shines into their hearts is 'the gospel of the glory of Christ' (v. 4) or 'the knowledge of the glory of God in the face of Christ' (v. 6). Therefore preaching the gospel is the divinely appointed means by which the devil's power in men's lives is overthrown and God shines savingly into their hearts. God's wisdom and pleasure are 'through the folly of what we preach to save those who believe'.[69]

But this proclamation, whether from a pulpit to a crowd or in a person-to-person conversation, will be effective only if the power of the Holy Spirit accompanies it. It does not matter if it is spoken in great human weakness, in fear and trembling, so long as it is 'in demonstration of the Spirit and power'.[70] Indeed it should always be thus, for it is only through 'earthen vessels' that 'the transcendent power' is seen to be God's rather than ours,[71] and only in our weakness that the power of Christ is made perfect.[72]

Such is the personal cost of a 'powerful' ministry. God does not share His glory with men, and, if we truly want to preach the gospel as the apostles did 'through the Holy Spirit sent from heaven',[73] 'not only in word, but also in power and in the Holy Spirit and with full conviction',[74] then we must be prepared to humble ourselves before God

[69] I Cor. 1:21.
[70] I Cor. 2:3, 4.
[71] II Cor. 4:7.
[72] II Cor. 12:9, 10.
[73] I Pet. 1:12.
[74] I Thess. 1:5.

111

the Creator as His weak and helpless creatures. Only when we truly glory in our weakness will the power of Christ rest upon us.

Many of the evangelists whom God has signally used have borne witness to the experience of being but a channel for the power of God.

Dr. R. A. Torrey, the American evangelist of the early part of this century, has explained how for years he refused to be a Christian because he feared that, if he surrendered to Christ, he would have to enter the ministry and become a preacher. 'But no one could be less fitted by natural temperament for the ministry than I. From early boyhood I was extraordinarily timid and bashful.' He went on to give examples of how shy he was in company, how after being converted and entering the ministry he would memorize his sermons, and how much he suffered. Then 'the thought got possession of me that when I stood up to preach, there was Another who stood by my side . . . and that all I had to do was to stand back as far out of sight as possible and let Him do the work. I have no dread of preaching now; preaching is the greatest joy of my life . . .'[75]

Dr. Billy Graham has many times spoken in similar terms. For example, addressing 2,400 ministers in May 1954, at the conclusion of the Greater London Crusade, he said: 'I have often felt like a spectator standing on the side, watching God at work. I have felt detached from it. I wanted to get out of the way as much as I could and let the Holy Spirit take over'.[76] And what gifted evangelists

[75] *The Person and Work of the Holy Spirit* by R. A. Torrey (Nisbet, 1910), pp. 73-75.
[76] Frank Colquhoun: *Harringay Story* (Hodder and Stoughton, 1954), p. 164.

like R. A. Torrey and Billy Graham have known can be the experience of the humblest Christian believer.

All this means that the supreme requirement in evangelism is to know more of the Holy Spirit's power. The first question which an evangelistically ineffective church should ask itself is: Why does the Holy Spirit appear to be bound? Is He grieved by our sin, or hampered by our unbelief? Do we need a deeper repentance, or more prayer?

Christ told His disciples to go and preach, but He also told them not to attempt to obey these commands until the Holy Spirit had come.[77] We do not need to 'wait' as they did, because we live after Pentecost, but we do need constantly to be seeking the same 'power from on high'. For Christ's promise is still true: 'If any one thirst, let him come to me and drink. He who believes in me, as the scripture has said, "Out of his heart shall flow rivers of living water". Now this he said of the Spirit, which those who believed in him were to receive . . .'[78]

CONCLUSION

The main feature of the biblical view of evangelism which we have been seeking to expound, in contrast to some modern evangelism, is its God-centredness. So in conclusion let it be said that our greatest need in evangelism today is the humility to let God be God. Far from impoverishing our evangelism, nothing else is so much calculated to enrich, deepen and empower it.

Our motive must be concern for the glory of God, not the glory of the Church or our own glory.

Our message must be the gospel of God, as given by

[77] Luke 24:47-49; Acts 1:8; cf. John 20:21-23.
[78] John 7:37-39.

Christ and His apostles, not the traditions of men or our own opinions.

Our manpower must be the Church of God, and every member of it, not a privileged few who want to retain evangelism as their own prerogative.

Our dynamic must be the Spirit of God, not the power of human personality, organization or eloquence.

Without these priorities we shall be silent when we ought to be vocal.

Simon Peter once found himself uncomfortably 'in the world', surrounded by the enemies of Jesus. They were in a courtyard on a cold, dark night, and had gathered round an open brazier to warm themselves. Peter was among them; it was a wonderful opportunity for witness. But when he was challenged by a little serving girl to declare himself a Christian he panicked and completely denied his Master. Three times he spoke in denial; three times he was silent in testimony. And when the cock crowed and Peter remembered the warning of Jesus, 'he broke down and wept'. They were the tears of chagrin for his guilty silence.[79]

We should not lightly despise Peter, for we share his guilt too often. Indeed we are altogether too ready to find a scapegoat for our own guilty silence, and to blame everything and everybody except ourselves. Yet our failure lies somewhere in our unwillingness to evangelize according to Scripture, to see God's gospel proclaimed by God's Church in the power of God's Spirit for the furtherance of God's glory.

It is to such godly evangelism that we humbly desire to summon the Church, and to dedicate ourselves.

[79] Mark 14:66-72.

APPENDIX 1

All Souls Church, Langham Place, W.1

COMMISSIONING SERVICE

Congregation sits. Candidates stand.

Minister to Bishop: I desire to present these persons to you, to be made Commissioned Workers in this parish.

Bishop: Do you believe them to be fitted for this work?

Minister: I have instructed them and have examined them, and believe them to be so.

Bishop to candidates: Do you believe that you are called by God to do this work?

Candidates: I do.

Bishop: Will you be faithful in the responsibilities you are undertaking, especially in prayer and loyal service?

Candidates: I will, the Lord being my helper.

Bishop: May the love of God the Father encompass you. May the presence of God the Son uphold you. May the power of God the Holy Spirit rest upon you. Go forth in the name of God, as the ambassadors of Christ and the servants of men; and may the Lord bless your labours abundantly.

Candidates: Amen.

Bishop: The Lord be with you.

Candidates: And with thy spirit.

Bishop: Our help comes from the Lord.

Candidates: Who made heaven and earth.

Bishop: The Lord will keep your going out and your coming in.

Candidates: From this time forth and for evermore.

Bishop: Let us pray.

All: The Lord's Prayer.

Bishop: Most merciful Father, send Thy heavenly blessing upon these Thy servants. Fill them with courage and humility, faith and zeal. Make them diligent in the study of Thy Word and dependent upon the power of Thy Spirit, and may the beauty of the Lord their God be upon them, for the glory of Thy Holy Name. AMEN.

All: The Grace.

APPENDIX 2

ALL SOULS CHURCH, LANGHAM PLACE, W.1

This is to certify that

....

having satisfactorily passed an examination

in the subject of the theory and practice of

evangelism has been solemnly commissioned

to serve as a Parish Worker of All Souls

Church, Langham Place.

Signed...............................
Bishop

....
Rector

Date........................

'Jesus said unto them, Come ye after Me,
and I will make you to become fishers of men.'
Mark 1:17

APPENDIX 3

ALL SOULS CHURCH, LANGHAM PLACE, W.1

Parish Survey

Male/Female Approx. Age......... Date...............

1. What is your occupation ?............... Nationality ?............
2. Do you live in this area ?   Yes/No

    If yes, how long have you lived here ?.....................
3. What contact have you had with our church ?

    All Souls Church ....

    All Souls Clubhouse ....

    All Souls Day School...

    St. Peter's, Vere Street ....

    If no contact: do you belong to another church or faith ?

    ....

    If some contact: is there anything you find hard to under-
    stand in our services ?...

    ....
4. Is there any way in which our church can serve this area
    better ? ....

    ....
5. What is your ambition in life ?...............................
6. Do you believe there is a God ?......... If yes, what is God
    like ? ....
7. Do you ever pray ?...

118

8. Do you read the Bible?...

9. What do you think sin is?...

10. Who do you think Jesus was?...

　　Why did He die?...

　　Do you believe He is alive today?...............................

11. How does a person become a Christian?......................

12. May I know your name?...

　　And address? ....

The Questionnaire concludes with the gift of this booklet. Would you read it?